DEVOTIONAL FOR CAREGIVERS

FINDING STRENGTH THROUGH FAITH

TERRY OVERTON

DEVOTIONAL FOR CAREGIVERS

Finding Strength Through Faith

Terry Overton

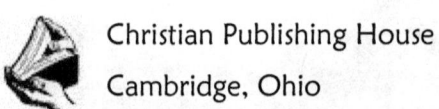
Christian Publishing House
Cambridge, Ohio

Copyright © 2018 Terry Overton

All rights reserved. Except for brief quotations in articles, other publications, book reviews, and blogs, no part of this book may be reproduced in any manner without prior written permission from the publishers. For information, write,

support@christianpublishers.org

Unless otherwise indicated, Scripture quotations are from the English Standard Version (ESV)

The Holy Bible, English Standard Version. ESV® Text Edition: 2016. Copyright © 2001 by Crossway Bibles, a publishing ministry of Good News Publishers.

DEVOTIONAL FOR CAREGIVERS: Finding Strength Through Faith

Authored by Terry Overton

This is a work of fiction. Names, locations, characters, and incidents are the product of the author's imagination.

ISBN-13: **978-1-945757-93-8**

ISBN-10: **1-945757-93-0**

In all things I have shown you that by working hard in this way we must help the weak and remember the words of the Lord Jesus, how he himself said, "It is more blessed to give than to receive" Acts 20:35

Dear Readers:

You may have suddenly found yourself in the role of a full-time caregiver, or the main caregiver, for a family member. This role is unique because it is full of daily challenges that you face as your put your own life on hold to care for another. This devotional book is unique because it focuses on topics that caregivers face in their day-to-day service to a loved one. These topics are ones experienced by the author and other caregivers of family members. Examples of the topics include understanding doctors' reports, everyday loneliness, maintaining your own energy levels, long nights, family support, and faith. These devotionals were written to apply to caregivers of family members with physically debilitating injuries, terminal diseases, mental decline, and life-long conditions of disabled children. The job of a long-term caregiver often goes without a thankyou or acknowledgement. This devotional serves to meet your needs and to illuminate the importance of your sacrifice. Your work is deeply appreciated.

Blessings to you as you continue your work,

Terry Overton

Table of Contents

Devotional for Caregivers: Finding the Joy in Pain 1
Nothing is the Same: The Day Your World Changed 2
Doctor's Reports 4
Disbelief 6
Why? The Unanswered Question 8
Crossing the Turbulent Sea 10
A Light in the Darkness 12
Eyes Look but Do Not Understand 14
Am I Alone? 16
Wondering About Their Thoughts 18
Struggling to Get Around Physically 20
Everyday Loneliness 22
Hope 24
Sadness 26
Whom Do You Turn To? 28
How Can You Talk to People? 30
Loneliness 32
What Was Once Done by Two Must Now be Done by One 34
So Tired...Please God Give Me Energy 36
Faith 38
Joy in Suffering 40
Feeling Imprisoned 42
Letting Professionals do Their Job 44
Priorities change 46
Feeling Anger Toward God 48

New Decisions...50
Things I Wish I'd Said 52
Longest Nights...54
Smaller World 56
Helpless but Not Without Hope 58
Time to Get Everything Done 60
Family Support...62
Resources to Meet our Needs 64
Nothing to Smile About...66
No Talking, No Sharing 68
Physical Dependence on Others 70
Basic Skills 72
No One Knows What I Am Going Through......................74
Finding Joy in Little Things 76
A Minute to Sit Down 78
When Your Efforts are Not Appreciated 80
A Different Person 82
Roller Coaster Emotions 84
Finding Time to Take Care of the Caregiver 86
Watching My Loved One Suffer 88
Wanting Answers 90
Changes in Medications 92
Well-Meaning Advice 94
Adjusting to Different Caregivers......................................96
Refusing Help..98
Accidents Happen 100
Quality of Life..103

Strength to Go Through the Next Phase 105

Is it Too Late to Grow Our Faith? 107

Peace 109

Being the Memory for Those Who Can't Remember 111

Prognosis 113

When Going to Church Seems Impossible......................... 115

Just Want Things to Be Like They Used to Be 117

Deep Depression and Sadness 119

When You Think It Can't Get Worse, It Does 121

Walking Through the Shadow of the Valley 123

Family Distancing and Differences 125

I Am Here for You (Even When I Need Some Rest) 127

God is Here 129

Recalibration of Happiness 131

Frustration 133

For Loved Ones with Terminal Diseases 135

Rejoicing Always... 137

Afterword 139

Appendix.. 140

OTHER RELEVANT BOOKS.. 150

Terry Overton

Devotional for Caregivers: Finding the Joy in Pain

Caregivers of loved ones are often overlooked in the scenario of long-term illnesses, lifetime debilitating injury, or fatal diseases. The importance of the work of the caregiver cannot be overstated. Taking care of a loved one with cancer, Alzheimer's Disease, a person involved in a tragic accident who sustained a debilitating injury, or a child with a lifetime condition requiring full-time support, can drain the energy and compassion out of any caregiver. The caregiver is often asked about the patient but seldom do people ask about the caregiver. This book is written for the caregivers who work day-in and day-out to support a loved one. The support provided can be spiritual or mental support, physical support to assist in daily functioning, taking the patient to appointments and therapies, hospital sitting, feeding, bathing, and any other type of care needed to help the individual with chronic or terminal conditions. If you are a caregiver, please use this devotional for your own spiritual support. If you are not a caregiver, but know someone who is doing this important work, pray for them and share this devotional with them.

DEVOTIONAL FOR THOSE COPING WITH TRAGEDY

Nothing is the Same: The Day Your World Changed

Have I not commanded you? Be strong and courageous. Do not be frightened, and do not be dismayed, for the Lord your God is with you wherever you go. Joshua 1:9

Joshua was set to enter into the promised land. This was his designated place in the history of God's chosen people. Knowing the role he was to play was not enough to make it happen. In addition to Joshua being the designee, God instructed Joshua that he needed to know God's word and to be strong and courageous. When Joshua followed God's command to be strong and to rely on Him, God would be with Joshua as he completed God's work.

In the scenario above about Joshua's role in entering the promise land, Joshua knew the expectations and that God would be with him. For those who support another individual with a chronic condition or terminal illness, the plans likely were not known to you in advance. Perhaps you learned of your new role as a caregiver in a doctor's office when you and your loved one were given the diagnosis of a disease. You may remember the exact words the doctor used to explain what was going to happen. The words may echo in your mind over and over for quite some time. At first, you may have reacted with bravery and put on a strong front for your loved one. Or, you may have felt the shock right to your core. You may have felt panic or anxiety. You may have gone to other doctors seeking another opinion, and that search proved futile. Different people process the initial news in their own way. However the news was given to you; you may have realized at that very moment in time, nothing would ever be the same again in your lives.

Upon hearing the news of your loved one, you may have felt frightened. Perhaps you did not know what to do next. Maybe you asked a few questions in haste, but the answers blurred together. You attempted to make sense out of the news, but it was difficult.

Like Joshua, we need to rely on God to walk through this initial difficult time. Reading Scripture provides guidance. We need to call on Him for our strength. Your world may have changed, but God never does.

You are my hiding place and my shield; I hope in your word
Psalm 119:114

The 119th chapter of Psalm is the longest chapter in the Bible. This chapter focuses on the important and sufficiency of God's word. It is notable that the longest chapter in the Bible tells us of the importance of following God's word to guide our lives. The Psalm above is a verse that simply states God is the hiding place and the protection from temptation or doing wrong acts. All hope is in the word of God. For those who have received unsettling news, you may be tempted to travel down a road of sadness and despair. Resist that temptation and rely on God for protection and strength as you as you work through these events in your life.

Heavenly Father, you are my hope and refuge in this difficult time. I ask for strength and understanding as we move through this new phase of our lives. Guide me with your word. Amen.

Doctor's Reports

Bear one another's burdens, and so fulfill the law of Christ Galatians 6:2

During the time Paul the Apostle was forming new churches and bringing new believers to Christianity, he provided instruction to the believers about how Christians should live. In the verse above, he was speaking to the believers in Galatia. Paul wanted to be sure these new believers understood that we are all here to help each other. This is what Jesus expects.

For caregivers who are supporting loved ones with chronic conditions, debilitating injury, or terminal illnesses, there may be multiple doctor's office visits. You may need to drive your loved one to various appointments and meet new doctors. Your role may include arranging for different types of diagnostic tests. Following these examinations and tests, the results are presented in doctors' reports, summaries, diagnoses, and images. Medical terms and reports may be confusing in a time when anxieties are already increased. At this point, a caregiver may feel that the medical personnel are moving too quickly to process all of the information that is piling on you. As a caregiver, you want to offer support and kind words, but since you are also confused and even frightened by what you are hearing, it may be challenging to cheerfully support your loved one who is sick.

Make me to know your ways, O Lord; teach me your paths. Lead me in your truth and teach me, for you are the God of my salvation; for you I wait all the day long Psalm 25:4-5

When you feel overwhelmed by the words, images, pages of reports, columns of numbers and lab results, take a breath and pause to collect your thoughts. The verses from Psalm above are a request for guidance from God through prayer and Scripture. In this chapter of Psalm, David told the people how to make sure they were ready to receive the word of God. He knew the importance of using the knowledge of God's word for guidance. This serves as a reminder that praying to God for guidance, reading Scripture, and taking some time to think about what is happening, may assist the caregiver and the patient. Ask the doctors and other medical professionals to explain or repeat their comments so that you can assist your loved one with making sense of the reports. Having this clear understanding will help when making any decisions that need to be made. Do not be afraid to ask questions. When you are told something in terms that you do not comprehend, ask the medical staff to define the terms so that you and your loved one both understand the meaning. Take notes and ask for clarification. Remember that your role, like the Galatians, and all Christians, is to serve others.

Heavenly Father, please help the doctors who provide us with information so that we may find the right interventions for this illness or condition. Grant us the strength and patience to seek the right path. Amen.

Disbelief

Fear not, for I am with you; be not dismayed, for I am your God; I will strengthen you, I will help you, I will uphold you with my righteous right hand Isaiah 41:10

The verse above by Isaiah, tells the people of Israel that God is always with them, even in their struggle. The people of Israel had been through many trials and were not yet in the land that God would later help them to regain. During the time of trouble for God's people, Isaiah reminds the people that all of their strength comes from God and He continued to watch and take care of them. Even in the worst of times, praying for strength will provide support for those who are frightened.[1]

Upon hearing tragic news that changed your life and the life of the patient, your first reaction may be one of utter disbelief. You may search for other answers. You may scour the internet looking for an expert or reading about diagnoses or therapies. When you heard the diagnosis, you and your loved one may not have believed what you were told. You may have felt shock, sadness, anger, fear, anxiety, and hopelessness. The verse above reminds us that even in the times of the greatest trouble, God will not leave us. We can count on God for strength and support. We can pray together and ask that God holds each of us in His hand.

It is the Lord who goes before you. He will be with you; he will not leave you or forsake you. Do not fear or be dismayed Deuteronomy 31:8

---

[1] RECOMMENDED READING
REASONABLE FAITH: Saving Those Who Doubt by Edward D. Andrews **(978-1-945757-91-4)**
REASONS FOR FAITH: The First Apologetic Guide For Christian Women on Matters of The Heart, Soul, and Mind by Judy Salisbury **(978-1-945757-43-3)**

When Moses could go on no longer, he handed the leadership role to Joshua. He told Joshua that he should not be afraid because God would not leave him, and he should not be discouraged. There may be times when you, as the caregiver, will need to take the lead for your loved one. You may be the one asking the questions and arranging for appointments. You may be the one who will ultimately decide when you can no longer take care of the loved one by yourself. You may be the one managing treatments and medications. As you and your loved one enter into an unknown part of your future, do not be discouraged. The road may be new, but you will not be traveling by yourself. Do not fear.

Heavenly Father, please give us the strength we need to travel down this new road of our lives. Help us to understand the condition and to find the best answers to our questions. Thank you for always being by our side. Amen.

DEVOTIONAL FOR THOSE COPING WITH TRAGEDY

Why? The Unanswered Question

Trust in the Lord with all your heart, and do not lean on your own understanding Proverbs 3:5

For as the heavens are higher than the earth, so are my ways higher than your ways and my thoughts than your thoughts Isaiah 55:9

The Bible includes many verses in the Old and New Testaments that call upon us to trust that God's knowledge is greater than our own.[2] Indeed, we cannot know how God thinks and why things happen as they do. The first verse above is written in Proverbs within a chapter that focuses on wisdom and how it will help us to live in our world. Here, wisdom means an understanding of the whole picture of God, His plan, and our place in that plan. This does not mean that we have God's wisdom, but rather that we study the wisdom in the Bible to learn about and respect the wisdom of God. This type of wisdom can guide us in our day-to-day lives. We rely on the wisdom presented in the Bible.

The verse above from Isaiah was written to warn the people of Israel that they do not know how God thinks and therefore they should not presume that they can plan as if they know how God plans. We cannot know the ultimate plan that God has for us. We can only trust that God's wisdom is greater than our own.

When you heard the news of the significant medical challenge facing your loved one, you may have spent countless hours asking why. Why us? Why did this happen? What caused it? Could we have done something different? Could this have been prevented? In

---

[2] Why has God Permitted Wickedness and Suffering?
http://bit.ly/2qHkwYR
Why is Life So Unfair?
http://bit.ly/2p43Ai9
Does God Step in and Solve Our Every Problem Because We are Faithful?
http://bit.ly/2qLdxgN

thinking about these questions, it is important to understand that in all of medical science, the reasons for a disease or condition to occur are usually unknown or at best, a guess about why the disease developed. Why does a person who partakes in a particular lifestyle, such as smoking or overeating, get a disease when another person, with the same lifestyle, does not? Why is one child born with a condition and another is not? Why does one person driving down an icy road have an accident when thousands do not? There are often many factors that contribute to an accident occurring, or the development of a disease or disorder, and these factors must be timed just so for the condition or incident to occur.

But is knowing the reason why going to make a difference in supporting the loved one with the condition? Probably not at all. In fact, worrying about the why questions can drain all of the mental, spiritual, and physical energy right out of a person. In times of worrying about why, you should turn your thoughts to God and ask for strength.

Seek the Lord and his strength; seek his presence continually! 1 Chronicles 16:11

This verse instructs us always to seek God for his strength. This means we praise God and ask for strength in tough times. Rather than always seeking the answers to why questions, seek God's strength continually.

Heavenly Father, we ask for your strength and wisdom to help us daily meet the challenges we face. Thank you for being with us during this time. Amen.

DEVOTIONAL FOR THOSE COPING WITH TRAGEDY

Crossing the Turbulent Sea

When you pass through the waters, I will be with you; and through the rivers, they shall not overwhelm you; when you walk through fire you shall not be burned, and the flame shall not consume you Isaiah 43:2

This verse from Isaiah reminds us that, just as God protected his loved people, the Israelites, He will be with us during rough times. God told the Israelites that no matter what they had to walk through, He would be there. They would not be destroyed by the water or flames.

As a caregiver, you may truly feel that you are crossing a turbulent sea or walking through a fire on any given day. You will have days of utter exhaustion, yet you will put on a smile and serve your loved one without fail. You will have days when you would rather be doing just about anything else than sitting by a hospital bed. You might daydream about taking a trip to a tropical island rather than taking a drive to the oncologist office, the rehabilitation center, or the memory care center. You will tire as you wait to drive your loved one home from a chemo treatment or from a dialysis center. On these days, you will wonder how much longer you can go on. And months or years later, you may realize that on this particular day, you had only begun this long-term journey as a caregiver.

What can you do now to give you strength? To keep your outlook fresh? To put on the smile and cheerfully ask your loved one what they would like to eat for lunch? To cheerfully change bed linens or wash clothes?

Behold, God is my helper; the Lord is the upholder of my life Psalm 54:4

You will need to steal away a few moments each day to sit in silence, take a deep breath, and be with God. Do not feel selfish about finding these few moments for yourself. To take care of your loved one, you will first need to take care of yourself. Your mind and body will require just a few moments of quiet in the chaos. If possible, make this time a routine time each day and then, if you can, take additional moments as you need them throughout the day. This time can recharge your battery. Take a moment, say a prayer asking for strength and thank God that you are also able to assist your loved one at this time.

Heavenly Father, once again I ask you to restore my soul. Please provide strength and energy that I need to help my loved one through this day. Thank you for providing me with the spiritual strength to help my loved one today. Amen

DEVOTIONAL FOR THOSE COPING WITH TRAGEDY

A Light in the Darkness

This is the day that the Lord has made; let us rejoice and be glad in it Psalm 118:24

When you read the verse above, you may not feel the joy and gladness. But it is true that since you are reading it, you have been blessed with another day. How that day will turn out, only God knows. But we know one thing is for certain: God, as the creator and giver of all gifts, has provided another day. Caregivers may not sense what is in store for the day. The schedule may have been planned out, but later, when you reflect on the day, you realize it turned out differently. As you put your weary body to bed, thoughts of why the day ended up as it did will spin through your mind.

The road a caregiver travels is often one of complex twists and turns. It is complicated because your world is now shared with a loved one in a way for which you were not prepared. Before the onset of the disease, disability, or condition, your life was more straightforward. Now, it may feel that you are traveling in a maze instead of down a neatly paved highway.

If you are just beginning this journey, you can rest assured that you will not be voyaging on your own. God is always there and will provide you strength and guidance when you ask Him. If you have been on this journey for some time, you have probably had days when you felt you were barely holding on to meet the demands. Remembering that God is your light when you hit bumps in the road will give you courage for each day. His love is stronger and more consistent than any other love we will ever experience. No matter what trials, tests, or blessings you encounter, God knows, watches, and loves you.

Try as you might, worry may still pop up. Worry is often a big part of being a caregiver. You worry about everything: if the doctor will give you the news you want to hear, if the medication or surgery will be effective, or if the meal you set before your loved one will not upset their stomach. There are plenty of worries to go around. But in all of the worry and darkness that you may feel from time to time, always remember the love that God has for you and your loved one. You never have to be is anxious about is God's love.

There is no fear in love, but perfect love casts out fear. For fear has to do with punishment, and whoever fears has not been perfected in love 1 John 4:18

The verse above reminds us that fear is not associated with God's love. Understanding and relying on God's love will ease our fears. The Apostle John told the readers of this letter that fear is associated with punishment and that God's love is beyond any fear. God can relieve fear, ease worry, and provide light for you to endure any dark places on your journey.

But let all who take refuge in you rejoice; let them ever sing for joy, and spread your protection over them, that those who love your name may exult in you Psalm 5:11

Because God eases our worry and fears, we can rejoice. We know that God will protect us and that the events that happen to you and your loved one are part of a larger plan that only God knows and understands. As a caregiver, you can ask for strength and protection at any time. Ask for calmness. Ask for peace. God will listen.

Heavenly Father, thank you for your constant love. Help me to remember your love and to grow my faith as part of the journey I am taking as a caregiver. Please give me guidance to help my loved one. Amen.

DEVOTIONAL FOR THOSE COPING WITH TRAGEDY

Eyes Look but Do Not Understand

For we walk by faith, not by sight 2 Corinthians 5:7

When Paul addressed the people of Corinth, he wanted to be sure they understood that our ultimate goal is to be with Christ spiritually rather than to be consumed by earthly concerns. He was speaking here about knowing that the new believers who had accepted Christ would eventually be with Christ in heaven. Paul was known as an Apostle with great skill in teaching and speaking. As part of this task, he wanted to make certain that others understood him completely.

As you spend time with your loved one every day supporting their needs, you may have times when you notice they do not understand what is happening. A loved one with Alzheimer's Disease may seem to look at you but not understand. A loved one who has suffered a stroke may look at you but not understand the words you say or may not be able to respond back to you. A child with a developmental condition may not understand everything that is going on in their world. A permanently disabled loved one suffering from brain damage may not be unable to comprehend as they did before the accident. Perhaps your loved one cannot remember anything that just happened, including the words you just spoke. Some medications may cause your loved one to interact differently or to not interact at all.

These difficulties with understanding and communicating can leave caregivers with a sense of loneliness. If you are truly to meet the needs of your loved one, it is unsettling when you cannot communicate to them in a way that you know they comprehend. You may struggle to find out what they want to eat, where they want to go, and what they want to do next.

Now faith is the assurance of things hoped for, the conviction of things not seen Hebrews 11:1

In the verse from Hebrews, the people were told that our faith needs to go beyond what we see. True faith means that we also believe in things that cannot be seen. When you are living, you cannot see heaven. But believing in the existence of heaven is a mark of your faith, your true belief in God, and in the grace given to us through Christ. Like the people with whom Paul spoke during his time of bringing people to Christ, we too, as caregivers must have faith. Our loved one may not be able to respond or comprehend as before, but we have faith that our love for our family member will guide us in meeting their needs. Perhaps they cannot tell you their thoughts, but you know their needs and can pray for guidance in meeting those needs.

Heavenly Father, thank you for your strength to help me meet the needs of my loved one. Please guide me in knowing what is best and in doing what my loved one wants. Amen

Am I Alone?

Be strong and courageous. Do not fear or be in dread of them, for it is the Lord your God who goes with you. He will not leave you or forsake you Deuteronomy 31:6

In the verse above, Moses tells Joshua not to be discouraged because God is always with him. More than that, Moses tells Joshua that he should not dread the future because God will be there with Joshua and the Israelites. The message of God being with His chosen people, guiding them, strengthening them, is a common theme in the journey to the promise land.

You too are on a journey that will be fraught with disappointments, challenges, and celebrations. At times, you may feel that God has left you. You may feel isolated from everyone and everything you knew before your loved one became ill. Like Moses, you will need to pray and have conversations with God about your fears and challenges you face. You are not alone, but you may have to remind yourself that God is always with you no matter what is happening.

Your loved one may also feel isolated and that no one cares about their well-being. Here is yet another challenge for you: to meet the needs of your loved one, so they do not feel alone. Together, you can work through the hard times and rejoice when you have small victories and celebrations for progress or times of peace.

Is anyone among you suffering? Let him pray. Is anyone cheerful? Let him sing praise James 5:13

The verse above was written by James, Jesus's brother. He was addressing believers, and he was concerned that they knew about their faith and could be set apart from those who challenged their faith. In this part of the chapter, he tells the believers that if they are ill or suffering, to ask for help and when things are joyful, they should praise God for that. Your joyful times may not be as plentiful as they were in the past, but you will notice these times. The condition of your loved one may actually cause you to pay more attention to the little things in life that bring joy. Perhaps once therapies or treatments are begun, you will have days when you can both stay at home and rest. These are the days to find something simple and joyful to appreciate. When you notice these little joys, share them with your loved one and give thanks for those moments during the time of great stress.

Heavenly Father, we know you are with us every day even though we may forget at times. Help us to remember that You are by our side. Thank you for the small joys you provide for us each day. Amen.

DEVOTIONAL FOR THOSE COPING WITH TRAGEDY

Wondering About Their Thoughts

Be still, and know that I am God. I will be exalted among the nations, I will be exalted in the earth Psalm 46:10

This Psalm seems to be a peaceful message when read as a single passage. What we must remember is that this was written to convey that, no matter what other battles were happening at the time between the people or nations, God would ultimately be victorious and would protect and save all who believed in him. God will always be the one in charge and will be held above everything mankind knows. This passage was written to offer peace and a sense of refuge for those who might be in fear of coming earthly events.

Caregivers worry. Caregivers have fears. Caregivers plan. Caregivers make phone calls, provide transportation, provide nourishment, and often assist in taking care of daily physical needs. During these times, caregivers wonder what their loved one might be thinking. Is their loved one worried? Do they have anxieties? Are they sad about their current condition? Do they worry for the caregiver? Do they harbor guilt about what has happened to them? Are they angry or upset about all of the appointments, plans, and dependence upon others?

Some caregivers may assume that they know what their loved one is thinking. Or, at other times, the caregiver may have no clue what is going on in their loved one's mind. Whether you feel you understand everything that your loved one feels, or you are completely in the dark, it helps to discuss this with the loved one whenever you can. If your loved one can respond, you will find their responses helpful. If your loved one is not able to respond, know that your loving care will result in peace of mind for you both.

Peace I leave with you; my peace I give to you. Not as the world gives do I give to you. Let not your hearts be troubled, neither let them be afraid John 14:27

Jesus spoke these words to his disciples not too long before he was turned over to be crucified. He wanted his disciples to know that they have no need to fear what was about to happen because they would be granted peace during this time of turmoil. He also wanted them to understand that the peace he was talking about was unlike any peace they had experienced before. This peace was the peace granted through the Holy Spirit and not the peace of this earth.

For caregivers who often worry about what their loved one is thinking, it is helpful to remember that the peace we gain by being Christian is peace greater than anything we can experience on earth. This peace goes beyond worldly peace and worldly understanding. Pray that your loved one also finds peace even in their suffering.

Heavenly Father, thank you for providing us with a peace that is greater than any worldly peace. Please remind us, that although we may not always know the thoughts of our loved one, we know that you care for us and will give us the strength to continue with our daily lives. Please help my loved one to feel your peace. Amen.

Struggling to Get Around Physically

He said also to the man who had invited him, "When you give a dinner or a banquet, do not invite your friends or your brothers or your relatives or rich neighbors, lest they also invite you in return and you be repaid. But when you give a feast, invite the poor, the crippled, the lame, the blind, and you will be blessed, because they cannot repay you. For you will be repaid at the resurrection of the just Luke 14:12-14

The Scripture above is from a story told by Jesus to inform his listeners that they should not worry about status of guests or about inviting people just so that they can pay back the invitation. More importantly, Jesus told this story to inform his listeners of the importance of providing service to the needy who cannot pay back the favor. Jesus used the examples of inviting people with disabilities, people who were too poor to pay you back, and people who were blind. He made the point to his listeners that service of this type was more important than our own gain we receive when we are paid back. In other words, service in which you do not expect to get paid back is the most honorable service you can do.

Your loved one may have a condition that weakens their body to the point that they cannot get around on their own. Perhaps they had a stroke and will need to learn to walk again if possible. Perhaps they suffer from cancer that requires debilitating treatments. Perhaps Alzheimer's has slowly stolen their physical strength and abilities. Perhaps a child has a developmental disability that requires multiple surgeries, or they are disabled for life. All of these scenarios present a person who is physically struggling to get around. As a caregiver, you will be the one who supports their physical needs and assists with ambulation or transporting them from one place (chair) to another (bed).

In using the infirmed in the story, Jesus let others know how important this work is. In fact, it is so important that Jesus said when you involve these individuals and include them as you serve God, you are considered among the righteous.

Let each of you look not only to his own interests, but also to the interests of others Philippians 2:4

During his ministry, the Apostle Paul suffered often, and he suffered harshly. Yet even though he suffered greatly, he did not pause for one moment to think that he should not serve Christ. He knew his suffering was for a greater joy. He told the people of Philippi that the final joy was through Jesus Christ. Paul wrote this letter while he was suffering himself, in prison. Caregivers should take heart knowing that looking after the interests of others is a primary expectation of all Christians. Helping those who cannot help themselves will bring you closer to God and to the joy that Paul knew in Jesus Christ.

Heavenly Father, thank you for the opportunities you have provided for me to serve others. I know that my loved one depends on me to assist in all matters of need. Guide me and provide the strength I need to serve others. Amen.

DEVOTIONAL FOR THOSE COPING WITH TRAGEDY

Everyday Loneliness

Be sober-minded; be watchful. Your adversary the devil prowls around like a roaring lion, seeking someone to devour 1 Peter 5:8

Peter wrote this letter to new believers to provide instructions about the Christian faith. In this passage, he was concerned that individuals who did not fully trust in God would stray from their faith and would behave as non-believers. His desire was to provide strength and remind the new believers of their role in staying alert to Christian living and expectations. He warned the people that if they did not pay close attention, they would fall away from their faith.

Caregivers may feel isolated and not supported by their friends and family. When you are tempted to feel sad, alone, or overwhelmed and overworked, know that God is with you always. Spend a few moments in prayer and then ask yourself about your own thoughts. Does it seem that many of your thoughts are negative? Do you sense that you are beginning to regret that you are the primary caregiver for your loved one? Do you sense you may begin to resent your loved one? Are you plagued by thoughts of spending time away from this loved one? Do you feel that there is no one who can help you? Are you feeling completely alone? Are you irritable around your loved one? These may be indications that you need a break in order to regain your strength and energy to take care of your loved one.

Having these types of thoughts does not mean you love your family member any less. These types of thoughts do not make you "bad person." You need to acknowledge these thoughts. Once you are aware of these thoughts, you can be watchful for their return, just as Peter told the new believers to be watchful. Your awareness can trigger you to take some actions to help regenerate your energy. Perhaps you only need a short walk outside to feel the fresh air and to observe God's wonderful creations. A few minutes spent watching a sunset or sunrise can have a powerful, uplifting impact. Watching children playing in the park, seeing your other family members and talking about other topics, can also provide you with respite and recharged energy. For these types of brief activities, your loved one can join you, or you can ask a family member or friend to sit with your loved one for an hour. This brief time away can provide a sense of renewal for you.

But may all who seek you rejoice and be glad in you; may those who love your salvation say continually, "Great is the Lord!" Psalm 40:16

This passage from Psalm reminds us that those who seek God will rejoice and feel that they have refuge in the Lord. When you are feeling stressed and need to take a few minutes or longer to be alone and have time away from your loved one, remember that God will be with you at that time also. We can rejoice knowing that He is always with us.

Heavenly Father, thank you for always being with us when we are tired and when we are working to serve you. Thank you for helping us to find a little time to renew our spirits. Continue to provide us with strength. Amen.

DEVOTIONAL FOR THOSE COPING WITH TRAGEDY

Hope

For in this hope we were saved. Now hope that is seen is not hope. For who hopes for what he sees? But if we hope for what we do not see, we wait for it with patience Romans 8:24-25

The Apostle Paul wrote this verse in his letter to the new believers in Rome. He conveyed much of the Christian doctrine in the letters he wrote to believers in the newly established churches. In this part of the letter, he is explaining what we know now as salvation in God's kingdom. We know that this will happen. We hope and wait for the day when we fully know eternal life in heaven. But we cannot see this yet. We know it awaits us and we must be patient.

In your role as caregiver, you know many periods of waiting. You are waiting for doctor's reports, test results, confirmation of health insurance payment, and waiting in hospital rooms and doctor's offices. Often your waiting will include hoping. You hope the doctor's report shows good results; you hope the medication is working, you hope your loved one will learn to walk or talk again.

As the verse above reminds us, we hope for what we do not yet know. One problem with our earthly hope is that it increases the likelihood we will also have worry. Worry can lead to anxiety.[3] This type of hope/worry/anxiety is not helpful to you or your loved one. Rather than have these thoughts running around in your mind night and day, you can turn the hope for earthly things into prayer. Pray that you and your loved one will rely on God and feel the peace that only faith can provide.

And now, O Lord, for what do I wait? My hope is in you Psalm 39:7

David, the psalmist, wrote this verse as part of a desperate plea for relief. David had many trials, including being chased and hunted by King Saul. David felt that he was being tested by God and asked

---

[3] How Can You Deal With Anxiety?
http://tiny.cc/lstqty

for God's help to overcome his situation. He realizes in the verse above that only God can help him, but he also knows he may have to wait for that help. In the interim, he placed all of his hope in God. He knew that only God would assist in his time of trial.

We see by this example, completely placing hope in God will bring help in times of trial. The help may be that we are able to wait patiently. The hope can also bring peace to your mind when waiting makes you anxious. When you find yourself waiting and becoming worried, it is best yo place all of your hope in your faith in God.

But I will hope continually and will praise you yet more and more Psalm 71:14

Heavenly Father, thank you for giving us peace to ease our worry. Please help me remember to turn to You for hope when I am waiting. Amen.

DEVOTIONAL FOR THOSE COPING WITH TRAGEDY

Sadness

The Lord is near to the brokenhearted and saves the crushed in spirit Psalm 34:18

The verse above states simply that God can save the spirit of sadness that dwells within a person who is feeling down. Being a full-time or highly involved caregiver of an individual who is dependent upon you, you will feel great sadness at times. Since the person for whom you care is a close family member, spouse, or another person with whom you have an important relationship, you will feel sad about their condition. You may also feel great sadness because you miss the way things were in the past when your loved one was able to participate fully in life. It is easy to go down the pathway of despair until you reach that destination of depression. Watch for any signs that you are spiraling downward into the pit of despair. If you feel the sadness is taking over your life, refer to the devotional on depression. If you are not able to pull yourself to a place that feels better through Scripture and prayer, let your Pastor or a counselor know right away. They are waiting to offer support that you need at that moment.

Although you may feel sad, there is much to be thankful for. Giving thanks is a great way to lift your spirits. It moves us from thinking of only bad thoughts to thinking about the bountiful blessings we have been given.

We are afflicted in every way, but not crushed; perplexed, but not driven to despair; persecuted but not forsaken; struck down, but not destroyed 2 Corinthians 4:8-9

The verses from 2nd Corinthians were written by Paul to the new believers in Corinth. He is telling the people there that things are bad, it is true, but things are not impossible. Paul reminds the believers that even though they are in a bad spot, they are not alone and that they do not need to fear because Christ has conquered death. As Christians, we know this to be true, and we have faith that we too will be with Christ in the end.

During the many weeks, months, or years that you are a caregiver, when you have episodes of sadness, remember that our hope and faith is in Christ. As you spend time with your loved one, be grateful to God for bringing the individual into your life. Be grateful for the time you have together and take opportunities to let the loved one know that you are glad they are with you now. It may be helpful to list all of the things you and your loved one enjoy doing together. You may also find it beneficial to write a list of the many blessings you and your loved one share. When you talk with your loved one, mention these activities and memories to lighten your spirit and to lift theirs as well. If possible, plan to do something enjoyable within the next day or two and take delight in sharing your plans with your loved one.

Heavenly Father, you know how my heart aches for my loved one. You know the sadness I feel at times. Please help my spirit and give me strength so that I can enjoy our time together. Thank you for bringing my loved one into my life. Amen.

DEVOTIONAL FOR THOSE COPING WITH TRAGEDY

Whom Do You Turn To?

That their hearts may be encouraged, being knit together in love, to reach all the riches of full assurance of understanding and the knowledge of God's mystery, which is Christ Colossians 2:2

When Paul wrote this letter, he was concerned that some of the brand-new congregations of believers might have been falling away from the true doctrine and may have been listening to false teachings. Why is this important to you as a caregiver? Paul wrote this part of the letter stressing that the love and fellowship that the believers felt toward each other and toward Christ would be strong enough to chase away any false beliefs. He felt that the connections the new believers had with each other would work to the glory of Christ and spread of Christianity.

This strong fellowship with Christians toward other Christians remains true today. Often times when Christians need support and help, they can turn to each other. Why? We can because we all have the same christlike worldview. We all understand God's grace and how much He loves us. This is a strong foundation that supports believers as they reach out to each other and it also is at work when we need to ask for help.

As a caregiver, you will likely meet many medical, psychological, and physical therapy professionals. All of these professionals have something to offer. In order to feel a real connection, if possible, find out which of the professionals are Christians and can support you with warm fellowship and care.

Connecting with other Christians, whether it is for medical assistance or transportation, nutrition, or a host of other needs, is important for another reason. Jesus made the following statement that is recorded in Matthew:

For where two or three are gathered in my name, there am I among them Matthew 18:20

As the verse above states, when there are two or more of believers together, there is Christ also. At this time of stress from multiple demands placed on you, it will be so encouraging to know that when Christians are together to accomplish something, or even just to support each other, Christ is there also. Jesus wanted us to know that feeling the presence of the Holy Spirit within two people who are in fellowship means that Christ is present. This will give you strength and comfort.

Heavenly Father, we thank you so much for sending your Son to take our sins away. We know that you love us and are present to support us in our time of need. Amen.

How Can You Talk to People?

Therefore encourage one another and build one another up, just as you are doing 1 Thessalonians 5: 11

In another letter from Paul, he wrote to the new believers that they should support each other, and talk to each other, for the purpose of cheering each other forward. He knew by being positive with each other; the church would grow stronger because the believers' faith would grow stronger. He felt strong churches and strong members would grow Christianity throughout the region. This is one reason that Christianity spread so quickly during that time period. The strength of the congregations aided in spreading the gospel.

During the days that you have experienced times of gloom, sadness, and stress, has anyone made a positive comment to you about what you are doing, the progress your loved one is making, or mentioned a positive acknowledgment? Did someone just say good morning and hold open a door? Did someone ask how he or she might help? When you heard the comment, although it may have been only a brief positive phrase, sentence, or question, did you feel that you were reinforced for your work? Did you feel a slight moment of cheerfulness or a change from your stress or gloominess?

With this in mind, have you made positive comments to your loved one? Or, have you made positive statements to others who are caring for your loved one? A positive remark, to build others up, has another effect. For the person making the positive remark, that person also feels a bit more cheerful. This is another way to think about the statement in Acts 20:35 that it is better to give than to receive. It may be hard on difficult days to think about something positive to say to someone. But as you try, you will be changing your frame of mind, on those tough days, from a frame of sadness or frustration to a frame of gratefulness. Be thankful for the other person assisting you, thankful for your loved one because you have shared time together, and thankful for a God who loves you so much that He provided grace to all believers. Gratitude is a terrific way to begin conversations and has positive feelings toward each other.

Behold, God is my helper; the Lord is the upholder of my life
Psalm 54:4

The verse above is a sentence that can help you to change your negative or gloomy perspective of thinking and look to our Lord, and remember, He is the source of our strength when times are difficult. He is the provider of our hope and always loves you. He will help to uplift your heart.

Heavenly Father, thank you for loving me so much and helping me on my tough days. Help me to remember a heart of gratefulness that will assist me in making positive statements to those in my life. Amen.

DEVOTIONAL FOR THOSE COPING WITH TRAGEDY

Loneliness

O Lord, all my longing is before you; my sighing is not hidden from you Psalm 38:9

The work you are doing is so demanding that you may have time for only a few social contacts or none at all. There may be many consecutive days when you see no one but your loved one for whom you are caring and healthcare staff. You may have days when you think you will never have any sense of normalcy or social company. Take heart and remember you are never alone. As stated in the verse above, if no one else is aware of your loneliness and pain, God is. We are so blessed with a God who always cares and knows our struggles.[4]

By this we know that we abide in him and he in us, because he has given us of his Spirit 1 John 4:13

The verse from 1 John is part of a pastoral letter that the Apostle John wrote to several churches of new believers. John included this sentence as one of reassurance. Keeping in mind that the Christian faith was fairly new, John knew that the believers might be tempted to follow false teachings or be persuaded by others who were attempting to convince the new believers that Christianity was not a valid faith. In this sentence, John reminded the new believers that God is always present with us. By saying that God has given us of his Spirit, John is stating that all believers can feel the love within our hearts once we received Christ.

On those very lonely days, take a few moments to think about God's presence in your heart. It is that presence in your heart that gives to others in service, such as being a caregiver. God's work is being completed through your hands. You are never alone.

There will be days when you strongly feel the need to have a social contact, if only for a few moments. On those days, say a prayer and then reach out to someone who understands your

---

[4] Can the Bible Help Us Cope With Loneliness?
http://tiny.cc/vyrqty

struggles. Contact members of your church, family members, friends, neighbors, a pastor, or local support groups who understand your place of service to your loved one. A phone call or a cup of coffee shared with another will recharge you. A walk with a neighbor, a chat with a pastor, can be great energy boosters.

Heavenly Father, thank you for being present with me always. I know you will give me strength and guide me to meet my longing for fellowship during these days of struggle. Amen.

What Was Once Done by Two Must Now be Done by One

For the moment all discipline seems painful rather than pleasant, but later it yields the peaceful fruit of righteousness to those who have been trained by it Hebrews 12:11

The situation in which you find yourself may have happened quickly. You may have received the news about your loved one's illness or condition when you were not anticipating any changes in your typical routine of daily life. Or, the condition or illness may have slowly progressed to the point where you are now the primary caregiver. In any event, you are likely being called upon to do the daily routine that the loved one used to be able to do. These new tasks may include cleaning the house, taking out the trash, paying the bills, keeping the yard, or managing business affairs.

During the first few days of your caregiving, you may not have thought about these additional responsibilities. These tasks may have snuck up on you. As your support of your loved one increased to include taking care of physical needs, you may be feeling overwhelmed. All of the new tasks may be dumped upon you without warning. And here you are now.

The verse above from Hebrews was written to let the new Christians know that all believers are disciplined, but this is for the glory of God. This does not mean that Christians are punished. The word discipline in this verse conveys a meaning of service or sacrifice. The early Christians were persecuted and had many trials to test their faith. For caregivers, this discipline is one of personal sacrifice and service that shows true Christian living. As the verse states, later you will be rewarded for righteous living and sacrifice you are making for your loved one.

For which of you, desiring to build a tower, does not first sit down and count the cost, whether he has enough to complete it? Luke 14:28

In the verse from Luke, Jesus is telling listeners about the cost of being a true believer. He asks the question about planning to remind the listeners that all good things that are accomplished are planned and then carried out to the end. For a caregiver who may be overwhelmed with all of the additional details of daily living, any planning you can do early may assist you as you provide this service to your loved one. There are support groups and online organizations for all types of illnesses and conditions. Many of these resources offer caregiver guides for planning things such as legal tips, finances, and so on. It is always helpful to talk with other caregivers who are experiencing the same day-to-day tasks and may have suggestions to help with your questions. Others, such as your pastor or friends with expertise in the areas of finance or planning or other needed matters, may be good sources of support.

Heavenly Father, thank you for your presence in my life. Guide me to meet the tasks at hand and to seek out resources that will help me be of service to my loved one. Amen.

So Tired...Please God Give Me Energy

Come to me, all who labor and are heavy laden, and I will give you rest. Take my yoke upon you, and learn from me, for I am gentle and lowly in heart, and you will find rest for your souls. For my yoke is easy, and my burden is light Matthew 11:28-30.

You have probably experienced many emotions since you began this journey as a caregiver. But of all of the emotions and feelings you experienced, tiredness or exhaustion may be the most consistent. Stress of any kind, good stress, and bad stress, takes its toll. An example of both types of stress is when you are tired from your caregiver responsibilities, and your family members let you know they are coming to visit for a few days. This is a combination of good and bad stress, and once they go on their way back home, you will be even more exhausted.

Jesus said the verses above when He was speaking to believers and those who did not yet accept Him. He was informing the listeners that He knew about the burdens they had on their shoulders. The burdens included the demands and toil of their daily lives and the burden of now being a believer when others might not accept Him. Other people might ridicule or even persecute the new believers. Jesus reminded the listeners that following Him, and having a closer relationship with God, ultimately would bring a different type of peace and rest. He knew that the new believers would have peace in their hearts and love for others. This type of love is what motivates you each day to put your feet back on the floor in the morning, rise, and get back to your role as a caregiver.

Your yoke or burden is heavy. You are working night and day and sometimes all 24 hours of the day are consumed. God knows all. He watches and cares for you. God understands your exhaustion and will provide you with the strength to endure and persevere.

But they who wait for the Lord shall renew their strength; they shall mount up with wings like eagles; they shall run and not be weary; they shall walk and not faint Isaiah 40:31

The verse from Isaiah reminds all of us that when we rely on God, when we trust that He will be working with us to help our loved one, we will be given the strength we need to complete our tasks. This verse also informs us that there may be waiting involved. As you know, God has His own timetable. So, we pray, wait, and continue in the service to others. When we do this and trust in God, we can soar like eagles in our faith.

Heavenly Father, thank you for loving me and providing me with endurance. I trust you to guide me and help me to give devoted service to my loved one. Amen.

Faith

That your faith might not rest in the wisdom of men but in the power of God 1 Corinthians 2:5

As caregiver you will feel harried from all the tasks that must be completed each day for your loved one. When you find that you scurry about for many hours of the day, exhaustion sets in, and you may begin to wander down a gloomy path of hopelessness. It may feel that it is easy to lose heart and not feel positive about the work you have been called to do.[5]

The verse above is part of the Apostle Paul's letter to the new believers in Corinth. As you recall, Paul was selected by Christ to spread the word of salvation as he grew the new faith of Christianity. During this time period, there were many skeptics who promoted their own interpretations of faith and others who preached false teachings. In this verse from 1 Corinthians, Paul tells the reader not to rely on what men say but rather to have faith in the power of God. Paul fully knew the power of God since he had been provided the assistance of the Holy Spirit to guide him as he taught new Christians.

---

[5] IMITATE ENOCH: Walk With God Even in Times of Difficulty (http://tiny.cc/s3rqty) PROTECTION FROM FEAR AND DOUBT: Ways to Deal with Doubts About God (http://tiny.cc/i4rqty) Do Not Waver In Unbelief About God (http://tiny.cc/o5rqty) Jesus kindly Said to Peter "Stop Being Afraid" (http://tiny.cc/m7rqty) You of Little Faith, Why Did You Doubt? (http://tiny.cc/w8rqty) Nothing Is Impossible for Those Having Faith (http://tiny.cc/pasqty) Saving Faith Produces Christlike Actions of Christian Service that Proves its Genuineness (http://tiny.cc/fesqty) What Can Help You to Stand Firm in the Faith? (http://tiny.cc/6fsqty) How Strong Is Your Faith? (http://tiny.cc/qhsqty) Be Courageous and Strong Through Your Faith (http://tiny.cc/hisqty)

Take a moment, as a caregiver, and pause to renew your own reliance on God. You will hear many things from a variety of sources about your loved one's health condition, and their fate. What you hear may be accurate or maybe just a guess about the future. At these times, rely on God and your faith in Him. The Apostle Paul wrote the verse below to the believers in Rome. He reminded the reader that faith comes from hearing, and believing, the words of Christ.

So faith comes from hearing, and hearing through the word of Christ Romans 10:17

To keep your faith strong, read the Scriptures regularly. By reading and knowing the words of Christ, your own faith will increase. If you are unsure of the best books to read in the Bible, you can begin in the New Testament with the Gospels. Here, you will review all of the teachings of Christ, and these will reinforce your existing faith.

And without faith it is impossible to please him, for whoever would draw near to God must believe that he exists and that he rewards those who seek him Hebrews 11:6

Heavenly Father, thank you for sending your Son to us. Please help me to keep my faith strong and remember your constant love for me and my loved one. Amen.

DEVOTIONAL FOR THOSE COPING WITH TRAGEDY

Joy in Suffering

Count it all joy, my brothers, when you meet trials of various kinds, for you know that the testing of your faith produces steadfastness. And let steadfastness have its full effect, that you may be perfect and complete, lacking in nothing James 1:2-4

In this letter by James, he tells the readers that turmoil, tests, and other trials they experience, will help them develop faithfulness, closeness, or strengthening of their attachment to God. James knew that the followers of Christ would be tested and persecuted. He knew they would suffer. Our suffering can increase our dependence and faith in God. Think about that for a moment. This suffering can be from your perspective as well as your loved one who is suffering. Your loved one is suffering from an illness or a condition. Your own suffering is because you see your loved one struggling. You also suffer for yourself as you toil each day sacrificing your own personal life and desires to take care of the needs of someone else. Your suffering is a measure of your faith when you cling to God for strength, and you find love in living the life of a Christian.

Blessed is the man who remains steadfast under trial, for when he has stood the test, he will receive the crown of life, which God has promised to those who love him James 1:12

James tells the believers that when they persevere under stress, and they continue to believe in Christ regardless of their trials, they will be rewarded with love and eternal life. This is the promise made by God about accepting His Son into our lives. For those who are caregivers of people who are suffering, you are demonstrating your love for Christ by serving as just as He did. You continue to love others and serve without ceasing. You know this will bring you closer to God and strengthen your faith and resolve.

The Lord is my strength and my shield; in him my heart trusts, and I am helped; my heart exults, and with my song I give thanks to him Psalm 28:7

The verse from Psalm reminds us that not only is God our strength, but He is our shield as well. He will be there to protect you and guide you when you are facing difficulties of providing service to your loved one. The difficulties may be in dealing with medical staff, finances, or finding time for yourself so that you can rejuvenate your motivation to serve. For all of these needs, we need only to pray and open our hearts and minds to the guidance that can be provided to us through God's Word.

Heavenly Father, you are the strength and protection that I need to support my service. Thank you for always being by my side and for giving me the guidance and strength I need each day. Amen.

Feeling Imprisoned

Do all things without grumbling or questioning Philippians 2:14

As Christians, we know that the verse above from Philippians is what we are supposed to do. We should carry on, no grumbling, and do the tasks at hand that Jesus would have done. We should help the weak, share with the poor, help the infirmed, and share the news of Christ with others. This verse from Philippians was written by Paul to explain how people of the new faith should behave. In part, this was to set an example for others so that they could better understand Christians and Christianity.

As a caregiver, even though you know you are not supposed to grumble about what you are doing, there are days when you just can't help yourself. Your mind strays down the path of resentment and bitterness. You may be asking yourself questions like, "Why can't the other relatives help out? Why is it always me? When can I get a break? Why am I trapped in this role?"

Your feelings, although justified when you know others could be available to help, are not helpful. When you find yourself asking these questions over and over in your mind, it may be time to take a brief break. You may need just an hour of doing something other than caregiving. Do not think this is selfish. In the end, when you take better care of yourself, you can take better care of the person who is in need. If possible, kindly ask another family member or neighbor or friend that you trust, to sit with your loved one for just an hour or so. Use that time to refresh your mind by doing something out of the ordinary that will help you to get a second wind.

If this is not possible, take advantage of the time when your loved one is resting, napping, or in a therapy or rehab session, to do something that will help restore your happy outlook. And when you feel those negative thoughts and questions creeping back into your mind, reframe those thoughts. "Why can't other relatives help out?" Might be reframed into "I have been given this role by God to be a caregiver because others may not be ready for this difficult task." "Why is it always me?" can be reframed to "God gives us exactly what we can handle and will help me when I ask for strength." The question of "When can I get a break?" Can be reframed to "I am going to plan a break for ___ day and coordinate with relatives who can provide that time to my loved one." The question of "Why am I trapped in this role?" Can be reframed to, "As long as I am with Christ and Christ is with me, I have freedom. I will pray and use the strength provided by God to figure out how I can have a time for refreshing my mind. Then, I can better serve my loved one and God."

To help you get started with these reframing or rethinking strategies, you can say the following verses to yourself and pray.

Now the Lord is the Spirit, and where the Spirit of the Lord is, there is freedom 2 Corinthians 3:17

Out of my distress I called on the Lord; the Lord answered and set me free Psalm 118:5

Heavenly Father, thank you for providing me with the strength to help my loved one to this point. Please continue to give me strength and refresh my mind with your Spirit. Amen.

DEVOTIONAL FOR THOSE COPING WITH TRAGEDY

Letting Professionals do Their Job

The way of a fool is right in his own eyes, but a wise man listens to advice Proverbs 12:15

Listen to advice and accept instruction, that you may gain wisdom in the future Proverbs 19:20

The verses above were written not as an insult, but to say that it is wiser not to speak immediately if you disagree with someone. As a caregiver, you may wonder what these verses have to do with your role. Unfortunately, being a full-time or major caregiver can cause some fraying of nerves between you and those with whom you interact with frequently. While there is no doubt that healthcare practices need to be monitored and documented by you, there are times when a caregiver may react too quickly to medical staff and this may result in tough interactions down the road. Although you are the "expert" about your loved one's preferences, as the second verse says, you may become wiser in the future by listening to what the experts are telling you or your loved one.

It is up to you to advocate for your loved one in certain situations. For example, if medical staff are discussing a particular medication with your loved one, and you know that is a medication to which your loved one has an allergy, you must advocate and make certain there is no misunderstanding. But there may be other times when a suggestion or instruction may be difficult to hear or just something that you do not prefer to do. In those cases, we should not react quickly, but think about what was said and why this recommendation is made for your loved one.

One caregiver said that she *finally* realized it was her place to let the medical professionals, such as therapists, doctors, nurses, do their job and that she should simply be a loving family member. The staff no doubt viewed her as a "helicopter caregiver" always hovering and insisting that her way was the right way. As Christians, be watchful and considerate to those who are helping your loved one.

I glorified you on earth, having accomplished the work that you gave me to do John 17:4

The words above, recorded in John, were spoken by Jesus in a prayer. He said this prayer as He neared the end of His ministry. He told his Father that He had accomplished all that He was given to do, to glorify God. As a caregiver, regardless of the work the medical professionals do, it will fall to you to take care of your loved one. In order to care for your loved one as a Christian, it is important to follow the example of Jesus and to do your work so that it glorifies God. In other words, as much as possible, speak like a Christian to all those with whom you interact. Work for your loved one as if you are working for Jesus. Interact with all others as a Christian. If you disagree with what is being said, take your time to respond and think through your words carefully. In this way, you will be gaining the most knowledge for your loved one about what is to be done. And if you are certain that your knowledge of your loved one and their medical history dictates that the advice should not be followed, advocate for your loved one in a kind way. Know your loved one's medical history well enough to be able to interact politely and effectively.

Heavenly Father, thank you for providing your Son to accomplish everything You asked Him to do. Thank you for providing medical staff to help me take care of my loved one. Please help me with understanding and knowledge of the medical treatments and remind me to be kind to others. Amen.

Priorities change

Put on then, as God's chosen ones, holy and beloved, compassionate hearts, kindness, humility, meekness, and patience Colossians 3:12

When your world has been rearranged so that you can take care of a loved one, all priorities change. Your life has been turned upside down in some respects. It is as if every day must be filtered so that the needs of the loved one are met first and, if there are things you need or want to do for yourself, you must first consider how this will impact the loved one before you can follow through with your own needs and wants. On many days, by the time you meet the needs of your loved one, you do not have the time or energy to do the things you wanted to do for yourself. This is a different kind of sacrifice that others may not understand. And all the while, you are to try and do all of these things with a smile on your face and a song in your heart. Paul instructed the Colossians to do just this: to put on compassionate hearts, kindness, humility, meekness, and patience. That is a tall order to continue this kind and patient behavior day after day. James, the brother of Jesus, wrote that those who are wise, and understanding, will have good conduct and that wisdom is evident in meekness. The meekness in this verse indicates that we will listen carefully, consider answers wisely, and react joyfully to what we hear.

Who is wise and understanding among you? By his good conduct let him show his works in the meekness of wisdom James 3:13

You probably do not know exactly how long your caregiving role will continue. You may be caring for a loved one who will recover soon from an operation, an injury, or illness that requires a number of different treatments. Or, you may be caring for a loved one who will require your support for the rest of their time here on earth. Until such time as your support will no longer be needed, you will be serving the loved one first before other duties of the day. Organizing and making sure your work is effective, will allow you to have more free time or down time, to rest or do other things. In addition to looking for support through online professional groups, you can make a list of things you must do each day and determine what sequence makes the most sense for you to be effective in your role. Before going out to run errands, make sure all of the tasks you need to do while out are organized for effectiveness and to save time.

By reading the paragraphs above, it is easy to realize that your priorities have indeed changed. The depth of the love you have for your loved one is evident. Your world now revolves completely around someone else. When you read the verse below, think about what John said about Jesus. We love Him because He loved all of us first. Jesus loves us so much that He died for us and freed us from our sins. In turn, we love each other and support each other as He asked us to do. So, while your life has been rearranged, remember the love you have in your heart for your loved one. That love is what is driving you to continue with your work. Jesus's love for us drove Him to the cross. In all of the work and turmoil you have, be thankful that God took care of us, too, by sending His Son.

We love because he first loved us 1 John 4:19

Heavenly Father, thank you so much for sending your Son for us. He showed us how to love and serve others. Please help me to continue to draw strength from your love. Amen.

Feeling Anger Toward God

As God lives, who has taken away my right, and the Almighty, who has made my soul bitter Job 27:2

If you know the story of Job, you know that he was afflicted and suffered over and over. He complained a great deal. He lost so many things in his life. He had poor health, he lost his children, and he lost his wealth. As a result of these trials he suffered, he was very angry. With all of the trials and tests that Job experienced, he even questioned why he was born. Whether you have been a caregiver for a long time or are just beginning, there may be days when you feel angry toward God. Job had many conversations with God and expressed his anger. In the end, Job's faith came through for him. Even though he was angry, he still had faith in God. Eventually, Job was richly blessed more than he had been in the past.

Caregivers may be angry[6] at times. Anger may first rear its ugly head when you hear the news of your loved one's condition. Anger may reappear as you trudge through many tasks that are difficult and trying for you. Anger may resurface when the wear and tear on your mental and physical state is felt. Anger comes when you have no time to yourself. Like Job, have conversations with God. Express your feelings and ask for help and strength. Read the Scriptures that bring you comfort. Take time with your loved one to do things other than caretaking responsibilities. Watch a movie together, go outside and enjoy the fresh air, have conversations about the many memories you already had together before the illness or injury happened.

Let love be genuine. Abhor what is evil; hold fast to what is good Romans 12:9

Paul wrote in his letter to the Romans to tell them that the love of Jesus is real. The love we share with each other as Christians should be real. It should be genuine. God's love for you is genuine,

---

[6] Let All Wrath and Anger Be Put Away From Us
http://tiny.cc/13tqty

and you can trust Him for strength and guidance during times of trial. Paul also wrote we are to hold tightly to everything that is good and loathe anything and everything that is evil. So, even when we are frustrated and angry, we are to hold on to our faith tightly, as Job did. We should keep positive, loving thoughts in our hearts and change our negative thinking to positive, loving thoughts for our loved one. Thinking positive thoughts may require time, silence and prayer.

Heavenly Father, forgive me when I am angry. Help me through the days of trials. Give me strength and knowledge when I am tested. Amen.

New Decisions

Follow the pattern of the sound words that you have heard from me, in the faith and love that are in Christ Jesus 2 Timothy 1:13

Caregivers may feel overwhelmed with the number of decisions that need to be made quickly. And sometimes, once a decision is made, it doesn't work out and you are faced with yet another decision. These decisions can be every day small decisions that your loved one would make if not ill, or they may be major decisions that will impact therapy or life functioning. These decisions weigh heavily on caregivers. If you have medical power of attorney, you may be asked to make all medical decisions.

The verse above written by the Apostle Paul is one of instruction. He is telling his young new believer, Timothy, a brother in Christ, to follow the wisdom that Paul has imparted to him. What was the wisdom? Paul reminds him all of these wise words were established by the faith and love of Christ and Christ's love for us. What does this mean for a caregiver making decisions? This means looking at all decisions first within the frame of being Christian and keeping watch over your loved one's interests first.

Decisions can be tricky because there may be other relatives who want to weigh in. Since you are the primary caregiver, it may be difficult to hear the opinions of others. But keep in mind, they are acting out of concern. The verse below can be helpful to you when others would like to participate in the decision-making.

Without counsel plans fail, but with many advisers they succeed Proverbs 15:22

In the earlier devotional about letting medical professionals do their jobs, Scripture included listening to others and acting wisely. The same holds true for working with family members who offer advice about decisions. Listen and do not react quickly. Take your time if you can to weigh things out. Politely state your reasoning so that relatives can understand why you are going to make a particular decision. Thank them for wanting to be involved. You may need them in the future.

As for you, brothers, do not grow weary in doing good 2 Thessalonians 3:13

Paul addressed this verse from 2 Thessalonians to some members of the congregation who were struggling. After he told them to stop fussing and to work hard for their cause, he added that they should not tire of doing good works. For caregivers, the same is true. Settle any unnecessary unrest between any family members working with you so you do not become frustrated with your task of caregiving. Work together. Keep things respectful, peaceful, and read Scripture for guidance.

Heavenly Father, thank you for helping me with the task I have at hand. Please give me the wisdom to make the right decisions for my loved one. Amen.

Things I Wish I'd Said

Say not, "Why were the former days better than these?" for it is not from wisdom that you ask this Ecclesiastes 7:10

The verse above, written by Solomon, is from the section of Ecclesiastes in which Solomon offers advice. This particular verse tells the reader that we cannot really know if things said and done in the past days, were better than current days. He reminds us that only God has all knowledge.

As we take care of someone who is ill, disabled, or injured, we are taking care of someone who is different in some way from the person they once were before the illness or injury. Following a debilitating accident or illness that may be chronic or terminal, we often think about the past times and wonder if we did all we could do for the loved one. We wonder if we said all of the right things when we were supposed to say them. We may also feel regret that we did not make our own feelings known to the loved one sooner. These thoughts may cross our minds, but thoughts such as these are not worth extended time or mental energy. As Solomon notes, we really don't know if the times of the past were better than now. We cannot know the things that God has in store for the future. We can certainly take the time each day with our loved one to have heartfelt conversations and share Scripture and pray together. As much as possible, time may also be spent doing the types of activities the loved one enjoyed before the injury or illness.

The lot is cast into the lap, but its every decision is from the Lord Proverbs 16:33

Proverbs remind us also that all decisions, our past and our futures, are not determined by us. We can make plans, but those plans may never come to fruition. What God has in mind will happen. In the case of your loved one, an illness or injury came along and now lives are changed. With these events, we have no choice. Moving forward, always consulting with the Scripture and praying to God, will lift us where we need to be. By reading Scripture, sharing time with your loved one, you will find peace and strength to continue your tasks.

For he will not much remember the days of his life because God keeps him occupied with joy in his heart Ecclesiastes 5:20

Here Solomon lets the reader know that, in the end, if we are faithful and strong in our beliefs, we will continue to have joy in our hearts. This is difficult to do during challenging days, but we know that Christ has taken away our biggest burden and we have security knowing that our future will be brighter. Everything we have ever known, or had, or will have, are gifts from God. This includes the gift of his Son. This is how much God loves us. Thinking of how wonderfully blessed we are will keep joy in our hearts.

Heavenly Father, I am so blessed. I know that even in the tough times and rough days, you have been my strength and have given me many gifts. Please help me always to remember you and to keep the joy in my heart. Amen.

Longest Nights

In toil and hardship, through many a sleepless night, in hunger and thirst, often without food, in cold and exposure 2 Corinthians 11:27

The Apostle Paul suffered for many years to fulfill his appointed mission to spread Christianity. This particular verse is one of a string of verses in which Paul describes his suffering. Before this specific line about his sleepless nights, hunger, and thirst, he wrote sentence after sentence about his being beaten, shipwrecked, chased, and many other tales of his suffering. After all of these events, he adds that he has anxiety about the churches he started and wonders if the people are holding on to their faith. Probably you have not been shipwrecked or beaten, but you have suffered, gone hungry, been thirsty, and had many sleepless nights, all in the effort to care for a loved one. Like Paul, you probably also worry about the loved one, and perhaps this worrying takes the place of sleep. When you find yourself worrying in the middle of the night, it may help to restore your peace of mind to read comforting Scriptures, such as the one below.

Do not be anxious about anything, but in everything by prayer and supplication with thanksgiving let your requests be made known to God. And the peace of God, which surpasses all understanding, will guard your hearts and minds in Christ Jesus Philippians 4:6-7

As stated by Paul when he wrote to the believers in Philippi, you should not be anxious about anything but should give thanks and pray. Pray for what you need and read and study the Scriptures. Paul added that in so doing, peace will come, and your heart will be guarded by the love of Christ Jesus.

With so much going on in your life as a caregiver, during hectic sleepless nights, it is hard to imagine that kind of peace. This requires trust and faith on your part. Of course, God can give you that peace. Just ask Him for it. Your strong faith and prayers will bring you the rest you need. Make it a priority to get enough sleep and rest each day. This will provide you with the physical strength and alertness you need to carry on with your role as caregiver.

In the verse below, Jeremiah tells the people of Judah that, after repentance for their sins, God will return to the people of Israel and will help the people to recover from their previous deterioration. He not only tells them they will be able to prosper but here Jeremiah adds that God will satisfy the tired and weary. He will replenish them. With strong faith and prayer, thinking about peace in Christ Jesus, He will also replenish you.

For I will satisfy the weary soul, and every languishing soul I will replenish Jeremiah 31:25

Heavenly Father, thank you for the many blessings you have provided. Please restore my peace of mind and replenish my energy. Please guard me against my worries and anxiety. Amen.

Smaller World

For I consider that the sufferings of this present time are not worth comparing with the glory that is to be revealed to us Romans 8:18

Some days may seem to be a blur. At times, it may feel like one day is no different from the next. Each morning you wake up to the same caregiving routine. You go through the motions. Perhaps your world has been reduced to the same number of chores, times for medications, meals, bathing and dressing, combing hair, and so on. The Apostle Paul wrote the verse above to the new Roman believers. They were being persecuted and suffered for their beliefs. Paul reminded them of the great gift of faith and the grace given to them, and this was greater than the suffering they were enduring.

Maybe before your loved one became ill or injured, you had become complacent in your faith. Like the new believers in Christ, we often need to be reminded that having a strong Christian faith is worth it. Being Christian rewards you by strengthening your spirit and energy when you are feeling down. Being a Christian means, you have the support of other Christians. You can call on others for assistance when you need it. If your world has become smaller because of the responsibilities you have as a caregiver, you can open your world up by asking others to come into your space and visit with you. Christians are willing to help each other. An invitation to come in for a meal, even if they bring the food in, will boost your spirit and your faith. If your loved one can participate in the meal with others, it will bring happiness to the loved one to be able to socialize with others as well.

When the days seem to be repetitive, it is the time to do something different. Vary anything that is reasonable. Ask your loved one if they have an idea of something they would like to do. This might mean watching a new movie, going for a quick outing with your loved one if they can do so, or reading something different together. You can always pick a new Bible story to read and see what you can glean from the text. For ideas, look at either minor prophet stories or others from the Old Testament. One interesting place to begin would be a book that includes miracles. Try looking into 1st and 2nd Kings. You will read about food being brought in by ravens; a boy raised from the dead, and prophets who multiply food, just to name a few. Another option for shaking up the routine might be listening to audiobooks. Audiobooks are a "hands-free" way to read a book together. This format will allow you to multitask as you listen.

During these testing times of repetitive routines, pray for strength. Ask God for guidance in selecting other activities that your loved one will enjoy. Be thankful for the time you spend with your loved one.

Many are the afflictions of the righteous, but the Lord delivers him out of them all Psalm 34:19

Heavenly Father, thank you for the strength You give me each day. Please help me to continue my work and provide me with the spirit and knowledge to always make the right choices for my loved one. Amen.

DEVOTIONAL FOR THOSE COPING WITH TRAGEDY

Helpless but Not Without Hope

For whatever was written in former days was written for our instruction that through endurance and through the encouragement of the Scriptures we might have hope Romans 15:4

Among the caregiving tasks that may fall to you, one may be to support your loved one so that they do not give up hope. It might be that they are struggling with difficult therapies such as physical therapies after an accident or chemotherapies for cancer. Or, it may be that they are fighting depression because their diagnosis has been deemed to be terminal by medical professionals. It may be that they are in the throes of Alzheimer's or dementia and they become frustrated, angry, or depressed because they can no longer do what they used to do and cannot remember what they knew. Cheering up and supporting your loved one can be difficult. As you struggle to do this type of caregiving, you may also feel helpless at times, not knowing what to do.

The Apostle Paul wrote the verse above in his letter to the Christians of Rome. He was providing them with instructions about Christianity before he visited the new believers there. In this verse, he wants them to understand that as new Christians, they were to study the writings of the past. These passages of Scripture from the past included many stories of the people of Israel and the endurance they had because of their faith. Knowledge of the years of suffering endured by others who were finally reaped their reward is uplifting and motivating for caregivers who must have endurance. We can have the same hope because of strong faith and the love of Christ Jesus.

The verse below from Psalm lets us know that the righteous, who are in need and pray to God, will be heard. It notes that God is especially attentive to those who are suffering and asking for help. This particular verse was one written by David when he had been captured and was afraid. He was so afraid when he was brought to King Achish that he faked being insane so that the king would release him. Now, he was desperate to escape! His scheme worked because of his strong faith in God. Indeed, David's prayers were heard.

Stories such as this, from the Old Testament, can be uplifting and interesting. These stories can provide hope to those who feel helpless.

The eyes of the Lord are toward the righteous and his ears are toward to their cry Psalm 34:15

After Paul reminded the Christians of Rome that they needed to study the Scriptures, he added the following verse. The idea of finding peace because you believe can uplift your spirits as well as those of your loved one.

May the God of hope fill you with all joy and peace in believing, so that by the power of the Holy Spirit you may abound in hope Romans 15:13

Heavenly Father, my heart, and mind sometimes become heavy. Please help me to find more joy by studying Your words. Help me to lift the spirits of my loved one. Amen.

DEVOTIONAL FOR THOSE COPING WITH TRAGEDY

Time to Get Everything Done

Come now, you who say, "Today or tomorrow we will go into such and such a town and spend a year there and trade and make a profit,"-yet you do not know what tomorrow will bring. What is your life? For you are a mist that appears for a little time and then vanishes. Instead you ought to say, "If the Lord wills, we will live and do this or that" James 4:13-15

In this letter written by James, the brother of Jesus, he tells Christians that we should always consider that our plans may not actually happen unless God wants the plans to be completed. God has the full picture of time and what will happen in our lives. We do not. James is also talking about time and how we plan ahead. Organizing and planning as a caregiver is an absolute necessity. Without planning and organizing, the routine does not happen, and appointments are not kept. Christian caregivers can plan and organize and ask for God's strength and guidance.

It may feel like you cannot be flexible with planning. Even with exceptional planning and prayer, plans may go awry. James reminds us God can change plans. Therefore, not only do we need to make plans, we should prioritize to get the most important things done first and think out a plan so that the tasks needed for your loved one can be completed.

James notes that our time here on earth is short. The time your loved one has with you may be very short. With this in mind, think about the joy and happiness you have now with your loved one, even in the frenzied daily routines and appointments. Sneak in a little joy, a little fun, a few smiles, kind words, every day that you share with your loved one.

So teach us to number our days that we may get a heart of wisdom Psalm 90:12

The verse from Psalm was a prayer to God because of the suffering and oppression of the people of Israel. The verse reflects the need to know how much longer the suffering would continue. Later in the chapter, the prayer of Moses states:

Make us glad for as many days as you have afflicted us, for as many years as we have seen evil Psalm 90:15

It is evident from the prayer of Moses, that wanting good days instead of bad days, and knowledge of how our time on earth will be spent, are not new concepts. As a caregiver, you wonder similar thoughts. You may feel that there is so much to do for the loved one and wonder how much time remains for your loved one. How many more days of pain and suffering before recovery or before the journey to our heavenly home? Whatever the amount of time or number of days, two things are certain: 1) we cannot know the number of days we have, and 2) our life on earth is short. Pray for joyous days and happy times. Take care of your loved one while you have the opportunity.

The heart of man plans his way, but the Lord establishes his steps Proverbs 16:9

Heavenly Father, I know my time with my loved one may be limited. Please guide me in the use of time. Help me to spend time wisely. Amen.

DEVOTIONAL FOR THOSE COPING WITH TRAGEDY

Family Support

And though a man might prevail against one who is alone, two will withstand him-a threefold cord is not quickly broken Ecclesiastes 4:12

When King Solomon was getting older, he wrote many words about his observations and advice. In the verse above from Ecclesiastes, Solomon was speaking to his people in an attempt to provide wisdom. He offered words about oppression and standing up for your beliefs and principles. Here, he was telling the people that it is better to work as a group because you are stronger, and you can withstand obstacles and hardships.

In your own particular family, you may be blessed to have multiple family members that can lend a hand and share the burden of caring for your loved one. More than likely, the full-time caregiving is left to you and maybe one other person helps out now and then. It is not always the case that other family members do not want to help, it is usually that they cannot help due to work hours, living a great distance away from your loved one, or have other family responsibilities, such as raising children.

You may unfortunately have other family members who could help but do not. In this case, it can get under skin. You may begin to resent that family member and, even worse, begin to feel jealous of their freedom and angry about your own situation. It will help to remember that you are given the opportunity to spend many hours with your loved one and this can result in you having a greater connection and stronger relationship with your loved one. You will have more conversations and shared time together.

The verses below were written by the Apostle Paul to two different congregations. These were instructions to the new believers who were working for the new church. In the verse from 1 Thessalonians, he is telling the congregation to let those who are lazy know that their efforts are needed. He instructs the people to encourage anyone who may be shy or not yet ready to work for Christ, to help those who are weak and, most important, to be patient. For you family members who may fall into these categories, it is wise to think about Paul's advice. The second verse, from Philippians, is directed to those who have the Spirit within them and are working for God's purpose. This is for the caregivers as well. Your heart is doing what God intends, to take care of others, help the weak, and look after your family. You will be rewarded for this good work.

And we urge you brothers, admonish the idle, encourage the fainthearted, help the weak, be patient with them all 1 Thessalonians 5:14

And I am sure of this, that he who began a good work in you will bring it to completion at the day of Jesus Christ Philippians 1:6

Heavenly Father, thank you for the opportunity to work for my family. Please give me patience with others who may not be as helpful. I ask that you also continue to provide me with the strength to do this important work. Amen.

DEVOTIONAL FOR THOSE COPING WITH TRAGEDY

Resources to Meet our Needs

Not that I am speaking of being in need, for I have learned in whatever situation I am to be content. I know how to be brought low, and I know how to abound. In any and every circumstance, I have learned the secret of facing plenty and hunger, abundance and need Philippians 4:11-12

As you may recall, Paul was called by Jesus to spread the news of His resurrection and grace. He traveled at least three extended journeys, establishing new Christian congregations, some in small homes, for a period of many years. During his travels, he only relied on God to meet his needs. This is why he wrote to the people of Philippi telling them of his own contentment, setting an example for all to follow. He tells the people that he has learned the secret of being content in all circumstances, no matter what. He found his contentment in being nearer to God, serving Jesus, and living the Christian example.

Your own situation may be difficult. As a caregiver, you may or may not have plentiful financial resources. Regardless of your previous financial status, what you find yourself facing now is more financial strain because of medical bills and the cost of care for your loved one. There are people available to assist you with financial counseling about medical bills at most hospitals and doctors' offices. It can be tedious and time consuming to think about how to juggle expenses for your loved one and still meet your own needs. Here again, do not hesitate to ask for help. These professional counselors can implement payment schedules and help you find resources to lighten your financial burden.

And my God will supply every need of yours according to his riches in glory in Christ Jesus Philippians 4:19

As Paul continues his letter to the people of Philippi, he lets them know that, with faith and prayer, their needs will be met. This does not guarantee money flowing in for your wants and your needs. This is speaking of finding the strength and courage with prayer and faith, to meet your needs and care for your loved one. This may also require some struggle and frustration on your part to make all of these things come together so that the finances can be managed. You may find it helpful to ask family members for assistance in this financial management. If you do not have family members who can help in this way, you can talk with people in your church or community that know about managing finance.

Heavenly Father, thank you for your many blessings that meet our needs for food and shelter. Please give me strength and wisdom to know the best way to handle all financial burdens of caring for my loved one. Amen.

Nothing to Smile About

The Lord is my shepherd; I shall not want. He makes me lie down in green pastures. He leads me beside still waters. He restores my soul. He leads me in paths of righteousness for his name's sake. Even though I walk through the valley of the shadow of death, I will fear no evil, for you are with me; your rod and your staff, they comfort me. You prepare a table before me in the presence of my enemies; you anoint my head with oil, my cup overflows. Surely goodness and mercy shall follow me all the days of my life, and I shall dwell in the house of the Lord forever Psalm 23: 1-6

The verses from Psalm 23 are likely known to you. In times when we feel we cannot hold up our heads, when everything seems dark, when we feel deep sadness in our hearts, these verses offer comfort. Here we see our great and wonderful shepherd pointing the way for us to go to a green, cool pasture, and rest. We are weary and downtrodden. But our Savior will warmly tell us not to worry. Rest. And then have a cool drink and be energized. He will provide strength and take us all the way we need to go for His name. All the way to our final reward. We need only to look at His staff as He walks along the path, leading us down the right trail, and we are comforted. We are tempted to become sad, angry, resentful, depressed. But our God tells us, "You may be walking near that evil. You may be tempted to take that path. But follow my staff and take my path. I am taking you to a feast of joy even though you are surrounded by that evil of darkness and gloom. Once we are at the table, I will bless you." And we know, our cup is not just full, but overflowing with God's love. Because He has poured so much love on us, surrounding us with his warmth and caring, we are going to have goodness in this life and the next.

The days of a caregiver can bring sadness. Your loved one has changed. Your life has changed. Your world is limited now to the day-in and day-out schedule, routine, appointments. But there is joy to be found in reading the Scripture and feeling God's word. Remember the Bible is a living book. It can keep you company and cheer you up on the days when you think there is nothing to smile about. Escape to it. Steal away 30 minutes and have the quiet time with God to renew your spirit and energize you for the day ahead.

But you, O Lord, are a shield about me, my glory, and the lifter of my head Psalm 3:3

This verse from Psalm tells us that God shields us. Just as in Psalm 23, we might be surrounded by the enemy: sadness. We might feel we cannot get away from despair. But we can. God will warm your heart and lead the way through His word. He will lift your head. You can count on it because He said it is so.

Heavenly Father, thank you for being here for me and with me. You protect me and cheer me in my time of need. I am so thankful for the energy you provide to me. Help me to remember Your word is my helper. Please fill me with the Holy Spirit. Amen.

DEVOTIONAL FOR THOSE COPING WITH TRAGEDY

No Talking, No Sharing

Do not cast me off in the time of old age; forsake me not when my strength is spent Psalm 71:9.

Your loved one may be elderly and non-communicative. Or, your loved one may have sustained injury that prevents communication, such as in a stroke or head injury. Perhaps your loved one does not have these types of concerns but does not share thoughts or feelings. If you are in the situation where your loved one, for whatever reason, is not sharing their thoughts or feelings, it can be more difficult to provide what they need. You may know their preferences for food, but other details of the day, such as what they would like to do, what they are feeling about the current situation, may go without answers.

You may also have questions about your loved one's thoughts about God if they are not able to talk with you. Perhaps your loved one was a Christian at heart before the illness or injury. You know from past experience that your loved one worshiped God and was in the right place in terms of their beliefs. Although you may not be certain if their feelings are the same now, you know their heart was filled with the Holy Spirit in the past, and therefore, the Spirit continues to be within their heart today.

But what if you were not sure about your loved one's faith? What if you did not know about their beliefs in the past? Should you share the Bible with your loved one not knowing how they felt about it?

For the word of God is living and active, sharper than any two-edged sword, piercing to the division of soul and of spirit, of joints and of marrow, and discerning the thoughts and intentions of the heart Hebrews 4:12

The verse above from Hebrews makes a clear point that the word of God is alive and continues to be active. This verse tells us that the word of God is so sharp and accurate, that it can pierce through into the soul of a person. The word of God can distinguish between those who believe in their heart and those who do not. It seems evident that the word of God should be shared with your loved one. If your loved one is a believer, the word can continue to have meaning for them even though they may not be able to respond to you verbally. If your loved one is not a believer, the living word can still be heard and perhaps understood and absorbed by the loved one. The Spirit can tell if the loved one has the intention within their heart to accept Jesus and the word of God.

The years of our life are seventy, or even by reason of strength eighty; yet their span is but toil and trouble; they are soon gone, and we fly away Psalm 90:10

As the verse from Psalm reminds us all, the years of our lives are soon gone, and we will join our God in heaven. Therefore, we should always study the Scriptures and live our lives as Jesus asked us to do. Share the Scriptures with your loved one, too.

Heavenly Father, thank you for the strength and guidance you give me each day. Please guide me to meet the needs of my loved one even when my loved one cannot speak to me. Amen

Physical Dependence on Others

He gives power to the faint, and to him who has no might, he increases strength Isaiah 40:29

If your loved one is suffering from a progressive disease, such as cancer or Alzheimer's, you may eventually see their physical strength decrease. This can cause you to feel a great amount of sadness since you knew the person they used to be before this progression advanced. The verse above speaks to the empowering word of God and the strength He provides to us.

For your loved one, there may not be any remission or return of strength and ability. This may tax you physically as you strive to meet their needs. You will physically need to help the loved one to different positions, travel to different rooms, and probably meet their hygiene and nutritional needs. You may need to learn how to use various types of equipment and administer a host of medications. All of this can wear you down even more than you were before. The verse above from Isaiah is for those, like yourself, who are tasked physically and become weak as you attempt to do the work you need to do. Isaiah wrote this to let the people know that even the very strong and healthy will become weak and will need to turn to God for strength to continue.

He will not let your foot be moved; he who keeps you will not slumber Psalm 121:3

As we struggle, by counting on our God and our faith, He will not let us fall. This verse from Psalm tells us that God will not sleep but is watchful. Even when we are weak ourselves and need rest, God watches over us night and day and will restore our strength.

My flesh and my heart may fail, but God is the strength of my heart and my portion forever Psalm 73:26

Even if we are weak and feeling like we are spent, God is the strength we have in our hearts to continue. When we feel the weakness, tiredness, and exhaustion creeping in, it is time for prayer.

Heavenly Father, You provide my strength each day. Today I feel tired and weak. Please provide me with the strength to continue my work and help my loved one with their physical strength and ability. Amen.

Basic Skills

Not many of you should become teachers, my brothers, for you know that we who teach will be judged with greater strictness James 3:1

It can be devastating to witness your loved one lose the skills they had before the injury or illness. In some cases, a loved one will need extensive therapy to learn to walk again, talk again, dress, and eat. In some cases, such as Alzheimer's, you watch these skills slowly slip away. The first time you hear a nurse or therapist tell your loved one, "Now let's put the food in the spoon," and the loved one still struggles, it can be heartbreaking.

The therapists and nurses who assist your loved one will probably recruit you, and maybe other family members, to provide similar instructions to your loved one. You will be teaching the basic skills of life that your loved one did with ease in the past. This may remind you of teaching a young child these simple steps only this process may require more time and patience. It may also be overwhelmingly sad. Yet, you know you must be enthusiastic and offer praise when your loved one is able to perform these simple tasks.

James wrote the verse above not to discourage people from wanting to become teachers, but because he understood the huge responsibility that teachers have. Teachers of the faith at that time were considered to be leaders of faith. As such, they were expected to be role models and were required to live to a higher purpose so that others would follow their example. James reminded those who wanted to teach that they would be held to a higher standard and examined closely by others.

Teaching these basic skills to your loved one may be frustrating at times. It may be depressing at times. But like the early Christians to whom James wrote, you must set an example for your loved one and for others who may be assisting you with caregiving. Being cheerful and encouraging will set the tone for the loved one that you care deeply and want them to be successful. This is also true if you must assist your loved one in these daily tasks for the remainder of their lives. Do so with a Christian heart.

Rendering service with a good will as to the Lord and not to man Ephesians 6:7

In this verse from Ephesians, the Apostle Paul is providing guidelines to the new believers about how they should work for the church and in life. He tells the Ephesians that whatever they do, they should perform the work as if it is for Jesus himself and not for another person. As you work diligently to assist your loved one, work as if you are helping Jesus himself, because you are. You are doing what Jesus would do.

And as you wish that others would do to you, do so to them Luke 6:31

Even though the tasks may be difficult, always remember that you may need someone one day. Treat your loved one, assist them, teach them, exactly as you hope someone would do for you.

Heavenly Father, thank you for the guidance of the professional staff as we work with my loved one. Help me to stay strong and to provide assistance with a cheerful, loving heart. Amen.

No One Knows What I Am Going Through

Give thanks in all circumstances; for this is the will of God in Christ Jesus for you 1 Thessalonians 5:18

Your burden has been heavy. Very heavy. You have been assisting and caring for your loved one for quite some time now. If you have read the previous devotionals, you have thought about your daily routines and missing activities of life before your loved one needed your help. You have read about asking for strength and guidance, making decisions, and working hands-on with your loved one and other professionals. You have likely longed for time to do something just for you. And after all of this, when you read the verse above about being thankful for all circumstances, you might think, "Seriously? I am to be thankful for this tough role I am fulfilling?"

In other devotionals, you read about working as if you are working to assist Jesus. You have read about having your heart full of joy for the time you have with your loved one. But it is still difficult. You have also asked, "Why?" And you have wrestled with so many questions and decisions.

But as you read the paragraphs above, can you think about why you? Can you answer the question "How can I be thankful?" The things you have been going through for this long period of time are difficult. So, with that in mind, who else do you suppose had the strength, the faith, and the love to do what you have been doing? Your answer is probably, "No one." So, how can you be thankful? You can be thankful that you have been given the strength and the wisdom and the faith to work through this role to this point. You can also be thankful for the sacrifice you are making for your loved one. You are doing something only you can do. God put this in your path of life, and you alone can carry out the task as you are.

Do not neglect to do good and to share what you have, for such sacrifices are pleasing to God Hebrews 13:16

Your sacrifice is known to God. The verse above was written to new Christians who no longer believed in making the animal sacrifices at the Jewish temple. They understood that sacrifices are good works we do for each other. We give these from the heart. We just may need additional strength to complete the tasks before us. And for this, the Apostle Paul reminded the Ephesians to use God's strength and might. When you feel that no one understands your circumstances, remember that God not only knows, He assigned this work to you. Be thankful. Pray. Ask for strength in body and spirit to continue the road before you.

Finally, be strong in the Lord and in the strength of his might Ephesians 6:10

Heavenly Father, thank you for providing me with the role of caregiver for my loved one. Forgive me when I am ungrateful. Help me to watch and care for my loved one with a cheerful heart. Amen.

DEVOTIONAL FOR THOSE COPING WITH TRAGEDY

Finding Joy in Little Things

Rejoice in the Lord always, again I will say, Rejoice Philippians 4:4

There are days when you may think you cannot feel joy. But you can. Observing God's bountiful gifts in our world brings joy to us all. Miraculous beauty in nature, the kindness of people you do not know, and watching your family members grow, flourish, and be successful. You may find joy in the most unexpected places and, at times, when you are caught off guard. Think about the nurse you spoke with who offered a smile and a fresh cup of coffee or the person who assisted you at the grocery store who smiled and helped you and told you to "Have a blessed day." And when you are struggling to find something to be joyful about, read the verse below from Psalm.

For our heart is glad in him, because we trust his holy name Psalm 33:21

This verse reminds us that our hearts can be glad because we have God in our heart. We trust Him and for this alone we can find joy. Remember that He alone has given you strength through your work. He has given you grace as an undeserved gift. He watches you and loves you always and no one can take you from Him. For these reasons, we have joy in our hearts because of His name.

As the Father has loved me, so have I loved you. Abide in my love. If you keep my commandments, you will abide in my love, just as I have kept my Father's commandments and abide in his love. These things I have spoken to you, that my joy may be in you, and that your joy may be full John 15:9-11

These verses from John were spoken by Jesus to the disciples. He was explaining to them that He loves us as much as His Father loves Him. Imagine that for a moment. God loves you as much as God loves Jesus. Jesus then stated that this should fill our hearts. Our hearts should be completely stuffed with gladness because God loves us that much. This is not a little thing in which to find joy. This is huge. But on your most troubling days when everything around you seems to be closing in, remember the love that God has for you.

You have put more joy in my heart than they have when their grain and wine abound Psalm 4:7

Heavenly Father, thank you so much for your endless love. You have truly blessed me with your love and your grace for me. Please continue to cheer my heart. Amen.

DEVOTIONAL FOR THOSE COPING WITH TRAGEDY

A Minute to Sit Down

Six days you shall work, but on the seventh day you shall rest. In plowing time and in harvest you shall rest Exodus 34:21

The verse above was written by Moses in the book of Exodus. In this book, Moses recorded the encounters that he had with God as he led the people through the desert. This is one of the instructions imparted by God to Moses. These were instructions to guide the people in their daily living. It is important to God that we rest. As recorded in Exodus, it does not matter the season of the year, we need rest.

As you read the passage above, you might have wondered how you could manage to have a whole day off each week. Sometimes it seems that you cannot even sit down for a few minutes to catch your breath. But resting is necessary for you to carry out your tasks. A few minutes rest can recharge you, energize you, provide you with a second wind. Finding time to sit can be challenging, but it is necessary.

Better is a handful of quietness than two hands full of toil and a striving after wind Ecclesiastes 4:6

If you realize that even with short breaks, you continue to feel tired and stressed out, examine your sleeping schedule to make certain you are getting to bed earlier enough and not waking up too early. As the verse from Psalm says below, it is not wise to have few hours of sleep.

It is in vain that you rise up early and go late to rest, eating the bread of anxious toil; for he gives to his beloved sleep Psalm 127:2

If possible, allow for a full night's rest. As you prepare to rest, read a verse or two from the Bible, and pray for rest. Put the thoughts of worry about tomorrow's duties out of your mind and think about the peace from God that surpasses all understanding.

If you lie down, you will not be afraid; when you lie down, your sleep will be sweet Proverbs 3:24

Heavenly Father, thank you for watching over me and sustaining my energy so that I may continue to serve my loved one. Please help me to put my worries aside. Amen.

When Your Efforts are Not Appreciated

Make a joyful noise to the Lord, all the earth! Serve the Lord with gladness! Come into his presence with singing! Know that the Lord, he is God! It is he who made us, and we are his; we are his people, and the sheep of his pasture. Enter his gates with thanksgiving, and his courts with praise! Give thanks to him; bless his name! For the Lord is good; his steadfast love endures forever, and his faithfulness to all generations Psalm 100:1-5

Reading the verses above from Psalm brings joy to our heart. These verses remind the reader of God's glory and goodness and that we all belong to Him. It tells us that we are His sheep and that we should be joyful knowing we belong to Him. We also know that He loves us always.

As a caregiver, you strive to meet the needs of your loved one. You may be the person who cooks and cleans as well as the one who takes care of the loved one's personal needs. You are probably with your loved one more of the day than not. You may be the one taking the loved one to all appointments and treatments. You may be the one who is responsible for administering all medications.

But what happens when the loved one, for whom you are working so hard and effectively, is not grateful? What happens when the loved one is angry or bitter about their circumstance, and they seem to take all of their anger and frustration out on you? You may feel at times like throwing up your hands and saying, "I can't do this anymore!". You may feel that nothing you are doing is working and that the loved one disapproves of the way you are handling everything.

There is no doubt that the loved one will become frustrated. They are dealing with new challenges and frustrations every day. If they lost strength or mobility, they might be tired of their physical limitations. If they are feeling ill many days due to an illness or treatments for cancer, they may be fed up with feeling sick and weak. Your loved one may have more bad days than good days.

Yet, you are making such an effort to have everything go smoothly that the reaction of the loved one can be exasperating to you.

As difficult as it may seem on those days, remember the examples that Jesus set for us about how we should serve others. The Apostle Paul wrote the following verses to the Philippians when he was giving them instructions on how to behave as Christians:

Do nothing from selfish ambition or conceit, but in humility count others more significant than yourselves. Let each of you look not only to his own interests, but also to the interest of others. Philippians 2: 3-4

If your loved one is angry every day, you may wish to have a thoughtful conversation about your own feelings. You might suggest coming up with some other system to for the loved one to communicate their feelings rather than talking angrily. You may also let your loved one know that you are trying very hard to be sure they are happy and comfortable, and you will continue to do so. Ultimately, there may be little if any adjustment in their attitude. It is difficult to keep joy in your own heart when you feel the loved one is so critical of your work. Continue your challenging job of working for the loved one remembering that you are providing a service as Jesus would do.

Take time to pray and read Scripture, like the verses from Psalm above that lift your spirits. Share uplifting Scriptures with your loved one. Keeping your heart cheerful and your mind aware of the difficulties your loved one faces may ease the tension. The heart of your loved one needs cheering as well. Pray that God can intercede and bring peace into the heart of your loved one.

Heavenly Father, thank you for sending your Son, Jesus, to show us an example of living like Christians. Please give me patience and love in my heart to endure and to lift the spirit of my loved one. Amen.

A Different Person

But the Lord said to Samuel, "Do not look on his appearance or on the height of his stature, because I have rejected him. For the Lord sees not as man sees: man looks on the outward appearance, but the Lord looks on the heart 1 Samuel 16:7

This verse is a passage in which God was instructing Samuel not to consider the appearance of people but rather to consider what was in their heart. Samuel had journeyed to find the future king of Israel. As he gazed upon some of the taller men, he thought perhaps God would choose one of them to be king. Instead, God instructed him to anoint David, the younger and smaller brother of a group of brothers. The verse was not written to let us know that height is not an important consideration, but rather outward appearance should not be the basis of judgment. We are to look at the heart of a person. Likewise, your loved one may have changed in looks and personality. God wants all people to judge others only on what is known in the heart.

If your loved one suffered a significant brain injury, stroke, Alzheimer's, or if cancer has now impacted their mind, God wants us to continue to pay attention to what we know is in the heart. The loved one you are caring for may have changed significantly in many ways. Their strength, skills, and mobility may all be different than before the illness or accident. These changes may require adaptations and physical supports to maintain health and meet their needs throughout the day. But perhaps the most challenging of all changes are those changes that happen in a person's mental state. This can include changes in their intellectual ability or personality. Their mood may be very different from your memories of their mood before the illness or accident. All of these changes can be very troubling when you are working hard to care and help your loved one.

For I do not understand my own actions. For I do not do what I want, but I do the very thing I hate Romans 7:15

The Apostle Paul wrote the verse above in a letter to the new Christians of Rome. In this part of the letter, he is informing the readers that evil is difficult to fight. He told these new believers that even when he is trying hard to resist sin, sin takes over his mind and choices and he sins when he is trying not to do so.

In the case of your loved one, even though you may have had conversations with your loved one about your feelings and their behavior, they may struggle to behave any differently. In the previous devotional, you read about loved ones who may not be grateful for your efforts. In addition to attitude changes or mood changes, your loved one may not be able to control some of their comments, outbursts, or behaviors. At times like this, think about what God told Samuel. Do not go by appearance, but rather remember what you know is in the heart of your loved one. They may not be able to show you or tell you about their heartfelt feelings, but you have memories and know them well from the past. Hold on to those pleasant memories so that you will have them to remember rather than any unpleasant behaviors.

Heavenly Father, thank you for telling all believers that we need to search the heart of people. Please provide me with the patience and understanding to care for my loved one when they have difficulty showing what is in their heart. Amen.

DEVOTIONAL FOR THOSE COPING WITH TRAGEDY

Roller Coaster Emotions

A fool gives full vent to his spirit, but a wise man quietly holds it back Proverbs 29:11

The verse above is one of many verses of advice that are included in Proverbs. The book of Proverbs, mostly written by Solomon, are nuggets of wisdom for all of us to read and apply. This particular section was written to advise leaders about their behavior. As stated, we should hold back from reacting or speaking when we are filled with anger and emotions.

Caregivers have many opportunities to practice holding back! For example, frustration with your loved one, waiting for services from medical staff, and last-minute changes in scheduling, snarky comments from your loved one, just to name a few. But it is important to hold back and remember that wisdom should prevail even when our tempers are hot.

During the many weeks, months, or years of your caregiving, you will have other opportunities to rejoice. When medical therapies are successful, when your loved one makes progress relearning skills, and when your loved one has a day of feeling happy and in better health, are reasons to celebrate. Likewise, you will have times of tears, such as a diagnosis you did not expect, the progression of a disease, or skills that are lost forever.

The verse below written by the Apostle Paul instructs Christians that these are the times to show emotions. These emotions, also known as empathy, show that you are walking in another's shoes. You are sad when they are sad and happy when they are happy. This is a way to show your support and closeness with your loved one. It also shows the tenderness of your own heart.

Rejoice with those who rejoice, weep with those who weep Romans 12:15

During your duration as a caregiver, you have no doubt experienced a roller coaster of emotions. These fluctuating feelings may continue unless your loved one stabilizes and eventually recovers. If, however, your loved one has a terminal diagnosis or chronic disorder that will not improve, your ride on the roller coaster may continue indefinitely.

Remember even when your emotions are variable, your love for your loved one should stay strong. Continue to let your loved one know you care. When you are tired or sad, work hard to spread cheer to your loved one, and you will find more cheer in your own heart.

Above all, keep loving one another earnestly, since love covers a multitude of sins 1 Peter 4:8

Heavenly Father, thank you for always loving me and holding me in your hands. Please keep me strong and help me to have patience and warmth with my loved one. Amen.

DEVOTIONAL FOR THOSE COPING WITH TRAGEDY

Finding Time to Take Care of the Caregiver

Or do you not know that your body is a temple of the Holy Spirit within you, whom you have from God? You are not your own, for you were bought for a price. So glorify God in your body 1 Corinthians 6:19-20

The Apostle Paul wrote this verse to the believers in Corinth. He wanted the people to know that they should not defile their bodies in any manner. He was specifically concerned that they might participate in sinful behavior that impacted their bodies in negative ways. Our bodies are gifts from God. As a caregiver, your concern for your body should be one of caring for your body and making sure you are receiving the nutrition and rest you need. This is important for you to consider not only for you but for your loved one. When you are in the habit of looking after someone else's needs every day of the week, it is easy to overlook your own needs. Being exhausted, anxious, sad, irritated, and short-tempered, are all side effects of not having proper rest and nutrition. When you, as a caregiver, are experiencing these negative moods, your thoughts become negative, and all of these added together will bring more tension to an already taxing situation.

Out of my distress I called on the Lord; the Lord answered me and set me free. The Lord is on my side; I will not fear. What can man do to me? Psalm 118:5-6

Taking care of yourself includes resting your mind. As a caregiver, you may feel a great deal of distress, anxiety, anger, resentment, frustration, as well as the positive stress such as celebrations of progress and sharing good days with your loved one. All of these emotions, and the frequent ups and downs of emotions, can be tiring. The more often you have these emotions, the more exhausted you may become. Likewise, the more exhausted you are, the more likely you will be to have negative emotions that will influence your level of care for your loved one. The better care you take of yourself, the better you will be able to care for others.

Though we speak in this way, yet in your case, beloved, we feel sure of better things-things that belong to salvation. For God is not unjust so as to overlook your work and the love that you have shown for his name in serving the saints, as you still do Hebrews 6:9-10

For all the hard work of a caregiver, you will be remembered and rewarded. The verses above tell us that in the future, better things will come to us because of God's grace and the sacrifice of His Son. We should therefore remember that the work of caregivers is another opportunity to strive to live as Jesus did. Living in this way is rewarded.

Heavenly Father, my days are long, and my heart and mind feel heavy. Please help me remember to take care of myself as I take care of others. Amen.

DEVOTIONAL FOR THOSE COPING WITH TRAGEDY

Watching My Loved One Suffer

Likewise the Spirit helps us in our weakness. For we do not know what to pray for as we ought, but the Spirit himself intercedes for us with groanings too deep for words. And he who searches hearts knows what is the mind of the Spirit, because the Spirit intercedes for the saints according to the will of God. And we know that for those who love God all things work together for good, for those who are called according to his purpose Romans 8:26-28

Watching a loved one suffer is very difficult. It is painful. You feel pain in your own heart for their suffering. It can be especially challenging if you know that their pain is chronic or if the pain is from a terminal condition or disease.

When you witness the pain of your loved one, it is hard to know what to pray about. Do you pray for the pain to stop? Do you pray for relief? Do you pray for endurance of suffering? Do you pray that their suffering is ended as they draw nearer to heaven? Do you pray that their journey to heaven is a brief journey? In these cases, we may not truly understand what we should pray. Are we praying these prayers to shorten our time of witnessing their suffering? Will the shorter journey make it easier for us as well as our loved one?

Caregivers of loved ones with these types of pain are torn. But there is no reason to worry about what you should pray. As the verses above state, we do not have to know the correct prayer. God, through the Holy Spirit, will know what we need to pray and will intercede for us. All we need to do is allow the Holy Spirit into our hearts completely. The pain is deep, and the Spirit knows our groaning. We can turn over the pain we are feeling for our loved one, and for our witnessing, to the Holy Spirit. The Spirit knows what we, and our loved one, will need.

As the verses, written by Paul, also tell us, the Holy Spirit knows the will of God. The Spirit knows the big picture and how all things work together for the good for believers in God, the Father, Son, and Holy Spirit. All things will serve His purpose, and we are but the instruments that He uses. It is tough for us to surrender this pain and suffering, to surrender the suffering we witness in our loved one, but we must. Caregivers must give this pain to God to be used for the purpose He has intended. We cannot know that purpose at the time we are suffering. All we can do and should do, is trust Him.

Let your steadfast love comfort me according to your promise to your servant Psalm 119:76

During the time of great pain and suffering, caregivers can be comforted by the love that God always has for us all. This has been promised to us, for accepting Christ and keeping our faith strong, we are comforted.

Heavenly Father, thank you for always loving me. Thank you for providing me and my loved with the endurance we need for this journey. Please guide me to meet the needs of my loved one. Amen.

Wanting Answers

But let him ask in faith, with no doubting, for the one who doubts is like a wave of the sea that is driven and tossed by the wind James 1:6

Caregivers have many questions. Initially, as you read earlier in the devotional, a caregiver will ask "Why?" Wondering why God allowed this to happen. Wondering why it has to be so difficult. Wondering why there has to be so much pain, hardship, treatments, weakness, are all questions asked by caregivers. These questions can keep you tossing and turning at night. These questions can make you bitter, angry, or anxious. These questions may tempt you to take that path of despair.

Perhaps the questions should be reframed into questions that reflect your faith. Rather than asking why this had to happen, reframe the question to a big picture question of how. How can this illness or injury bring light to others? How can this difficulty, pain, hardship, bring about a stronger faith in you, your loved one, and the people interact with each day? As the verse above tells us, if we have doubt in God or in our faith, we will be aimlessly tossed about, and we will find no peace. Continuing to hold tight to God's hand, will bring peace. Keeping strong in your faith and trusting that God knows the path for us will bring peace.

And so, from the day we heard, we have not ceased to pray for you, asking that you be filled with the knowledge of his will in all spiritual wisdom and understanding Colossians 1:9

The Apostle Paul notes that he, and other believers, began praying for the people in the church of Colossae as soon as he learned about their needs. In this case, the people of Colossae were being tempted to follow teachings that were not within the true Christian doctrine. Paul prayed that they would be filled with wisdom about the true understanding of God and Christ Jesus.

Like the new believers, we can be tempted to have errors in our beliefs or to question without true understanding. We might question why or question why me, why my loved one, when we are not feeling the strength of our faith. When we are tired and feeling drained, we may also become drained mentally and spiritually. When we are having doubts, when our faith feels weak, we can pray to be filled with spiritual wisdom and understanding that God wants us to have in our hearts and minds. By trusting in Him, we will have peace. When you have peace in your heart, you can better serve your loved one.

Heavenly Father, thank you for not giving up on me even when my faith is weak. Help me to trust you each day and to find peace through trust. Amen.

Changes in Medications

The grass withers, the flower fades, but the word of our God will stand forever Isaiah 40:8

Caregivers witness many things in their role. You will witness pain, sorrow, anxiety, the progression of the disease, a decline in skills, regaining skills, to name a few. One thing that can be quite troubling to caregivers is drastic observable changes due to changes in medications. Often times medical staff quickly go over side effects, or worse, give you a piece of paper with side effects and ask you to initial that you were made aware.

As a caregiver, you may notice subtle changes that will not be detected during an office visit or visit by a home health care nurse. You might see your loved one sleeping more or sleeping less. You will notice changes in appetite. Most troubling is a change in mood or behavior. For any change you notice, you will want to document and discuss with medical staff. It might be helpful to note how quickly the onset of the side effect occurred, how long it lasted, and when and if it subsides. Noting the time of day of medication and time of the beginning of a change in behavior will be useful to have during your next meeting or phone call to the doctor.

The true conflict occurs when the side effects are known, but you have to weigh the cost and effect of the medication. In other words, the cost, or side effect, is drastic but must be experienced in order to obtain the effectiveness of the treatment. Probably the most well understood of this cost and effectiveness reasoning is with chemotherapy. All who are involved know and understand the side effects of hair loss, weakness, nausea, but these are outweighed by the curing of the disease.

There are many other medications that are administered in which the cost and effect are not known or understood. Medications impact people differently. What impacts one person will have no impact or side effect on another person. This is when the caregiver can be the most helpful. Note any changes that you see in your loved one and let the medical staff know what you noticed. It might be that the medication is the correct one but the dosage needs adjusting.

No matter how the behavior of your loved one might change, remember that you know their heart and you also have a good idea about their daily habits of sleeping and eating. This is the trust that God has placed in your hands; you knew what your loved one was like before the illness and before the change in medication.

As the verse from Isaiah states above, many things change, but God and the word of God will always be the same. This we can trust. When you are going through troubling times of witnessing changes in your loved one and working with medical staff, it can be tedious and worrisome. Relying on God, and the Scriptures will bring you comfort. Reading the word of God will strengthen you and bring you peace.

Cast your burden on the Lord, and he will sustain you; he will never permit the righteous to be moved Psalm 55:22

Heavenly Father, thank you for the Scriptures that comfort and sustain me. Guide me as I work with medical staff. Help my loved one as we work to find treatments. Amen.

Well-Meaning Advice

If any of you lacks wisdom, let him ask God, who gives generously to all without reproach, and it will be given him James 1:5

The book of James, written by the brother of Jesus, begins with an opening chapter that focuses on having strength in faith and your beliefs. The verse above tells all who believe that if you are in doubt about your knowledge or wisdom of God, to pray about it. By praying for wisdom and strength of faith, you will receive this.

There will be numerous times throughout your caregiving role that you will be given advice. Some advice will be from the members of the medical profession. No doubt their advice is based on many years of education and experience. As a caregiver, you will want to make certain you thoroughly understand exactly what the professionals are advising. In earlier devotionals, it was suggested that you take notes and ask questions. This holds true when the staff is giving you advice. You can then discuss all options with your loved one, pray, and reason out the best course of action.

In addition to medical staff, you will hear advice from others who mean well. Sometimes these are other loved ones, neighbors, or friends. They may be inclined to tell you about their experience with their loved ones or, even their own personal experience about an illness. This information is interesting and may give you some ideas about what to expect or other questions to ask medical staff. This is one way that we, as humans, show empathy for others. We want others to know we know about their pain and suffering. This alone can feel helpful. It is always nice to know about another person who had a successful outcome. It is less helpful to hear about unsuccessful outcomes. These outcomes provide another perspective on what to expect. It may be realistic for the type of illness your loved one is experiencing. But always remember that only God knows the outcome at this point.

James continued giving advice in chapter 3. This chapter provides guidance on how to keep faith strong and, with strong faith, how to listen and speak to others. In this chapter, James tells the reader that listening to the wisdom from God is the key for peacefulness.

But the wisdom from above is first pure, then peaceable, gentle, open to reason, full of mercy and good fruits, impartial and sincere James 3:17

It is with peace in your heart, and a firm belief that God is wise, that you listen to others. In earlier devotionals, you read about the wisdom of listening and waiting to respond. When well-meaning people provide advice that is not welcome, it is best to let them speak their mind about the subject and then respond with respect. Although in your own mind you may be telling yourself that the individual has no idea what is going on with your loved one, it is better not to sound disrespectful. After all is said and done, you will want to keep their friendship. Remember that they mean well.

Heavenly Father, thank you for guiding me while I am caring for my loved one. Thank you for friends and family who try to help me by sharing their feelings and advice. Remind me to react as Jesus did and to be kind to others. Amen.

Adjusting to Different Caregivers

All the ways of a man are pure in his own eyes, but the Lord weighs the spirit. Commit your work to the Lord, and your plans will be established Proverbs 16:2-3

If your loved one has been dealing with illness, injury, or a condition, for an extended period of time, you may have already experienced interactions with other caregivers who assist you. These caregivers may be professionals who are trained in home health care or in specific therapies. They may be relatives or neighbors who provide respite for you. Or, you may share caregiving with others in shifts throughout each day. If you began as the first, or primary caregiver, you and your loved one might have had to make adjustments to others. Perhaps you trained others in the administration of medication or other therapies. If so, you worried about their effectiveness in doing the job you have been doing all along. Was the medication given at the correct time? Were the medical procedures followed for therapies? Did the other person carry out the task as expected? Were they as effective as you have been?

In some cases, the loved one may let a caregiver know when the correct procedures or medication was not administered. In some cases, if your loved one prefers that you are the caregiver, they may complain about others. Or, it may be that you loved one talks at length about the wonderful treatments administered by the other caregiver and, in fact, they could teach you a thing or two. In all matters dealing with other caregivers, it is wise to remember the verse above from Proverbs. The Lord knows the spirit, namely, the mental disposition within each person. God knows the wonderful work you are doing, and He will continue to make plans for you.

As with other conflicts, it is wise to take your time in speaking to either the other caregiver or your loved one about any adjustments that need to be made. The other caregiver may not be clear on specific instructions. The other caregiver may need to have directions repeated or written down in a sequence. And in dealing with all other people, we know that we are to be respectful and pray for guidance.

All Scripture is breathed out by God and profitable for teaching, for reproof, for correction, and for training in righteousness, that the man of God may be competent, equipped for every good work 2 Timothy 3:16-17

In all situations of caregiving, we can always turn to the Scripture for help an inspiration. In a letter that the Apostle Paul wrote to Timothy, his student, and believer in Christ, he told Timothy that since all Scripture is from God, it can be used in many ways. In the verses above, Paul told Timothy that we can rely on Scripture for our training so that we become competent in our work and we can continue to do good work. This is applicable to caregivers. By depending on the word of God, you can receive inspiration, strength, and knowledge to help you in doing our good work.

Heavenly Father, thank you for bringing other caregivers to help my loved one. Please provide me with the guidance needed to continue to work for my loved one. Amen.

DEVOTIONAL FOR THOSE COPING WITH TRAGEDY

Refusing Help

For the Holy Spirit will teach you in that very hour what you ought to say Luke 12:12

Jesus said the verse above to his disciples as He was telling them about the future. In this part of the book of Luke, Jesus warned the disciples that they would experience interrogations by the high priests and other authorities. These people in high places would question the faith of the disciples and would accuse them of blasphemy against God and the synagogue. But Jesus knew, because of the disciples' strong belief and acceptance of Jesus Christ, that the Holy Spirit would assist them in their time of need. Jesus wanted the disciples to trust their beliefs and to trust their faith. He knew that, even under a great deal of pressure, they would know what to say when the questions were asked.

When a loved one refuses help, the caregiver can be in a tough spot. The refusal might be of a new medication, a surgery, a treatment, or recommended diet. It is astounding to think of the many times during your caregiving role; you have had to use wisdom in talking with your loved one. When the loved one refuses help, you will need wisdom once again.

An intelligent heart acquires knowledge, and the ear of the wise seeks knowledge Proverbs 18:15

One thing that the Scripture reinforces across many different books in the Old and New Testaments is the theme of seeking wisdom before speaking. This verse from Proverbs reminds us not only to listen but to seek answers before making any decision. When a loved one refuses help, a therapy, treatment, or medication, weighing out the pros and cons will be useful. Speaking to medical staff about medical decisions is necessary. While the opinion of the medical staff is needed, it is even more important that you ask your loved one about the reasons for refusing the intervention or help. Perhaps there is an aspect of the treatment they do not like that can be changed. Perhaps the medicine they refuse makes them nauseous. If so, ask if there are other medications to treat the side effect or if the medication can be administered at a different time of day or in different dosages? If there is a therapy they do not want, ask your loved one to explain why and if there is anything that can be changed that might make the therapy more tolerable. These questions can then be asked of the medical staff as they work to find a new solution.

Teach me good judgment and knowledge, for I believe in your commandments Psalm 119:66

Caregivers who have the knowledge and wisdom about the treatments needed for their loved one will need to use good judgment in making decisions. In the Psalm above, note that the author is asking to be taught good judgment and knowledge because they have faith. We should rely on our faith and ask God for the guidance to use sound judgment when making these difficult decisions. Caregivers can pray for guidance when considering the benefits of administering or withholding treatment.

Heavenly Father, thank you for your guidance and support. Please be with me and assist me in making the best decisions for my loved one. Amen.

DEVOTIONAL FOR THOSE COPING WITH TRAGEDY

Accidents Happen

For you formed my inward parts; you knitted me together in my mother's womb. I praise you, for I am fearfully and wonderfully made. Wonderful are your works; my soul knows it very well Psalm 139:13-14

Our bodies are wonderfully made by God. The human body is fascinating from conception throughout life. All systems generally operate smoothly allowing us to grow, mature, have children, and live productive lives. Once the aging process begins, it can be a different story. Slowly but surely, the body begins to lose strength, flexibility, and endurance. Try as we might, we cannot stop the aging process of these wonderful bodies.

For your loved one suffering from disability, disease, injury, or a condition, the body does not work as it used to. This is frustrating and disappointing to your loved one and perhaps members of the family. But as a caregiver, by this point, you have figured out how to best support your loved one. You and your loved one have been getting through the days of appointments, therapies, and daily living.

When things are running smoothly, you begin to feel the rhythm of the routine. You may have the schedule down for you and your loved one and many days go without a hitch. And then an accident happens. Accidents can be falls, broken bones, mishaps with equipment or furniture, or bowel or bladder accidents that suddenly are occurring. These unexpected bumps in the road can be time-consuming, require medical attention, and can be embarrassing for your loved one. If the accident that occurred involved a new injury, this may cause a setback in therapies, treatments, and general progress. Now there may be another "new normal."

Your hands fashioned and made me, and now you have destroyed me altogether. Remember that you have made me like clay; and will you return me to the dust? Did you not pour me out like milk and curdle me like cheese? You clothed me with skin and flesh, and knit me together with bones and sinews. You have granted me life and steadfast love and your care has preserved my spirit [breath; life] Job 10:8-12

When Job was tested and suffered for so long, he became bitter and questioned God because he had a series of awful things happen to him. He yelled at God and felt that he was being punished. In the verses above, Job is questioning God. He asks God if He was not the one who created him and made him enjoy life at one time. After several chapters of anger directed toward God, God answers him and shows him the wisdom of God's ways. God explains that He does not punish people but created our wonderful world and our bodies and our lives. Then God explains creation miracles and wonder after wonder. At that point, Job repents and says the following verses:

Then Job answered the Lord and said, "I know that you can do all things and that no purpose of yours can be thwarted. Who is this that hides counsel without knowledge? Therefore I have uttered what I did not understand, things too wonderful for me, which I did not know Job 42: 1-3

Like Job, you and your loved one may feel that you are suffering one tragedy after another. Your loved one may become disheartened like Job. It may be difficult to keep the big picture in mind, that all things are working for a bigger plan. To maintain faith and strength during such trying times is difficult. As a caregiver, you may feel overwhelmed once again. You may think thoughts that question why your loved one has to endure so much.[7] You too may suffer because of the accidents that happen.

Only when Job was answered by God and realized the magnitude of God's power, God's miraculous knowledge, and the endless love that God has for all man did he remember his own faith. Like Job, we must do the same. We must remember the power, knowledge, and love that God has for us. Additional accidents,

---

[7] Why has God Permitted Wickedness and Suffering? (http://bit.ly/2qHkwYR); Why is Life So Unfair? (http://bit.ly/2p43Ai9) Does God Step in and Solve Our Every Problem Because We are Faithful? (http://bit.ly/2qLdxgN)

tragedies, or setbacks, should not sway us from our strong faith in God the Father, Son, and Holy Spirit. Review the Scriptures and pray for strength and guidance to meet the needs of your loved one.

Heavenly Father, thank you for your power, knowledge, and love. Guide me and strengthen me to serve. Please protect and help my loved one through this setback. Amen.

Quality of Life

This is my comfort in my affliction, that your promise gives me life Psalm 119:50

For loved ones who are suffering and experience setbacks, strong medications, surgeries or additional procedures, or accidents and tragedies, they may begin to think about their quality of life. As caregiver, you may also wonder if your loved one is happy and persevering through all of these procedures and incidents. When these procedures, medications, and surgeries continue for a long period of time, it can drain both the loved one and the caregiver. Each procedure or new medication requires an adjustment in the schedule, planning, and typical daily life. Additional follow up appointments, conferencing with medical staff, and learning to administer new therapies or medications, add to your burden.

The verse from Psalm notes that believing in God and knowing the ultimate reward we have through Jesus Christ, will comfort us. This is comforting for both the loved one and the caregiver. It may bring cheer to the loved one to read Psalm and other verses from Scripture that are uplifting.

My flesh and my heart may fail, but God is the strength of my heart and my portion forever Psalm 73:26

At these times of struggle, God is our strength. Reading about the life that Jesus had on earth can remind us of His suffering for us so that we can conquer death. We gain strength knowing that the price for any wrongdoing has been paid by Jesus. In this, we can be confident. Reading these passages and knowing we are free for eternity is uplifting.

Truly, truly, I say to you, whoever hears my word and believes him who sent me has eternal life. He does not come into judgment, but has passed from death to life John 5:24

Jesus said to her, "I am the resurrection and the life. Whoever believes in me, though he die, yet shall he live" John 11:25.

DEVOTIONAL FOR THOSE COPING WITH TRAGEDY

Although the quality of life on earth may change for your loved one, there is joy waiting in the future for us all.

Heavenly Father, thank you for sending your Son to take my place. Thank you for the grace you give to us as a gift. Please help us to stay strong in our faith and lift our hearts. Amen.

Strength to Go Through the Next Phase

Therefore we must pay much closer attention to what we have heard, lest we drift away from it Hebrews 2:1

Caregivers who work with a loved one for an extended period of time know one thing for certain: things change. Some of the changes may be good, such as making progress in a new therapy or rehab of physical movement. Some changes will not be good, such as declining mental or physical skills, the progression of a terminal illness, or changes in mood or communication. In all things, you may be preoccupied with making needed accommodations and adjustments in support.

For caregivers who are working with loved ones with terminal and chronic conditions, the future changes may have been explained to you by medical staff. You may have read about such changes on the internet or other medical sources. Friends who have had relatives with similar conditions may have told you of their own experiences. Some of the differences that you have heard are coming may not seem too drastic until you witness the actual change in your loved one. You may not be prepared for the impact the change will have on their behavior or skill. You may have thought about how your support will need to be modified, and then you might be taken aback when these changes happen.

With so many adjustments and modifications taking place, it is easy to become absorbed in thinking and planning for your loved one. In all things, as the verse from Hebrews above states, do not stray from your faith and your close walk with God. In fact, at this time, it may be more important than ever to remember what you have read and heard from the word of God.

Your loved one may have another bout with frustration or depression as their skills or abilities fluctuate. If your loved one has been cooperative and cheerful before, this is a time when you witness changes in attitude. Along with other changes in behavior, they may take out their frustration on you. Remember that it is not what they mean to do. You just happen to be in the room at the time. Also remember the wisdom of letting the loved one vent, talk, scream, yell, or otherwise react while you listen. As you listen to any complaints or outbursts, if possible, identify the main issues of the complaint and ask if there is anything you can do. Can you assist with positioning or medication to ease the pain? Help with the transition to a wheelchair? Aid with bathroom issues, or other concerns? Even if there is nothing else you can do to help, your loved one will know that you are patient and you are continuing to love them and serve them.

With all humility and gentleness, with patience, bearing with one another in love eager to maintain the unity of Spirit in the bond of peace Ephesians 4:2

Heavenly Father, thank you for your kindness and love for us. Help me to be patient and supportive of my loved one as they go through this transition in their condition. Amen.

Is it Too Late to Grow Our Faith?

This says the Lord: "Stand by the roads, and look, and ask for the ancient paths, where the good way is; and walk it, and find rest for your souls. But they said, 'We will not walk in it'" Jeremiah 6:16

The verse above from Jeremiah was written during a time of conflict between the people who believed in God and followed the teachings and the people who would not follow the Scriptures. Here, God tells the people to make a choice, noting that there is a good path and one that is not following God. He encourages the people to take the correct pathway and there they will find peace and their souls will find rest. In this particular part of the book, the people refused God's suggestion. They said they would not take the path to God.

Caregivers who are supporting a loved one with weak faith, or one who has profoundly stated all of their life that they have no room for God or the church, have a very difficult task. If you find yourself in this situation, you may also begin to question your own faith because of the constant tension that may exist between you and your loved one. Your loved one might be more bitter or resentful about their condition than those who have strong faith. Their disbelief can begin to take a toll on the caregiver.

As in the case of the people in Jeremiah who refused to take the right path, you cannot force your loved one to read Scripture, go to church, listen to church on TV, or any other action that they do not want to do. In fact, attempting to force the issue may cause more strife and conflict. Paul made the following recommendation to the people in Rome about those who were weak in their faith:

As for the one who is weak in faith, welcome him, but not to quarrel over opinions Romans 14:1

You may worry about your loved one's ultimate future. It may be difficult to realize this is not in your hands. You can, however, continue to live the example that Jesus asked us to live. Your behavior, your voice, the words you utter, can all reflect Christian living. And of course, pray for your loved one's heart and spirit to be moved closer to God. Pray that, even on their last day on earth, your loved one will accept Jesus.

But to all who did receive him, who believed in his name, he gave them the right to become children of God John 1:12

In this verse from John, it is clear that anyone who believes can make the choice to be in the kingdom of God. But they must first make that move. You can pray that they will.

Heavenly Father, thank you for the opportunity to accept your Son and to be a child of God. Please give me the wisdom to guide my loved one if possible. Please enter their heart and help them strengthen their faith. Amen.

Peace

Now may the Lord of peace himself give you peace at all times in every way. The Lord be with you all 2 Thessalonians 3:16

The Apostle Paul wrote the verse above to the congregation in the church of Thessalonica. The focus of this letter was to tell the people of the joy that would be experienced when Christ returns. Paul shared the news of Christ's resurrection, and conquering death, everywhere he went. His assignment was to spread the good news and start new churches. Here, he tells the people that because they believe in and accept Jesus, they will live in peace all of their lives.

It is hard to remember the joyful feeling of peace through Christ on days when you feel that you are in over your head. Caregivers frequently have those kind of days. Instead of feeling peace, you feel frazzled, nervous, frustrated, irritated. But feeling peaceful? Not on those days.

It will be helpful to find a few minutes of time to sit, take a deep breath, and remember your focus as a caregiver. You are serving your family member to make their life easier. Remember that God called you to this post and you will find joy in your work.

Aside from the possible physical work required of a caregiver, your role requires mental stamina and energy. A boost of energy can occur when you are free from anxiety and worry. As a caregiver, you know that worry and anxiety tag along on most days. This is why peace in heart and mind are needed. You cannot have true peace when your mind is loaded with worry. As difficult as it may seem, turning over your worries to God will help you to gain the peace you need.

Casting all your anxieties on him, because he cares for you 1 Peter 5:7

The Apostle Peter addressed the elders of the early church in this section of 1 Peter. Here, he is telling the leaders of faith that they are the shepherds of the flock of believers and that God knows they are willing to serve others. God knows of their work and their work will be rewarded so they should not worry but know that they are loved by God for this work.

As a caregiver, you too are doing the work that you are called to do. Your service is an example of living a life as Christ would want you to live. When your days are tough, remember that you are living a Christian life and performing a service in Christ.

What you have learned and received and heard and seen in me-practice these things, and the God of peace will be with you Philippians 4:9

Paul did not write the verse above to tell readers to imitate him because he was such a good Christian. He wrote this verse to the Philippians to remind them that in living a Christian life they would find peace, as he had. Caregivers are practicing a Christian life and peace is yours when you seek it earnestly with your heart and mind.

Heavenly Father, thank you for sending your Son to us so that we may have everlasting peace. Help me to turn my worries over to You so that I may find peace in my heart. Amen.

Terry Overton

Being the Memory for Those Who Can't Remember

The Lord God has given me the tongue of those who are taught, that I may know how to sustain with a word him who is weary. Morning by morning he awakens; he awakens my ear to hear as those who are taught Isaiah 50:4

In the verse above from Isaiah, the people of Israel had drifted from God and had suffered greatly. Many of the people of Israel became angry and frustrated with God because of their suffering. They were so involved in their complaining; they did not see the God was still waiting for them to come to Him in faith. Isaiah was stating here that he knew the words of God and he was ready to help persuade others who were complaining. He wanted to use what he knew to bring the people back to listening to God. He wanted to help them strengthen their faith. Isaiah's faith was strong, and he trusted God. He would use the knowledge that God had provided to help move the people back to their faith.

Like Isaiah, your faith is strong as you continue to serve your loved one. You have the knowledge of the word of God, and you have the knowledge of your loved one's history. Memory can fail us for many reasons. A momentary lapse happens to most people now and then. Your loved one may have other memory issues. Whether the memory is failing from dementia, Alzheimer's, brain injury, deterioration due to cancer or other progressive illnesses, or fading memory due to strong medications, you may have to be their memory. You can aid in their struggle to remember through the use of pictures, music, reading books, and other visual or auditory aids. Just as Isaiah mentions, you may need to do this day after day. Isaiah listened to God morning after morning. You may need to repeat things to your loved morning after morning. As their loving caregiver, they trust you. As our loving caregiver, we trust God to continue to bless us with strength and guidance as we do our work.

Let us then with confidence draw near to the throne of grace, that we may receive mercy and find grace to help in time of need Hebrews 4:16

Witnessing the memory loss of your loved one can be difficult. It is when we face trials and challenges that we should rely on God even more. At the time of the writing of Hebrews, Christians were being persecuted for their faith. They were challenged with staying strong in their faith and possibly facing severe punishment or even death. As noted in the verse from Hebrews, these early Christians were told to be confident when they prayed to God. Even with the extreme challenges they faced, they needed to remain strong in their beliefs. Like these early Christians, we should pray with confidence to God so that we can receive strength and guidance in our time of need.

Heavenly Father, thank you for always being here for me. Please help me to remain strong in my faith as I work with my loved one. Guide me to assist my loved one with their memory. Amen.

Prognosis

In the day of prosperity be joyful, and in the day of adversity consider: God has made the one as well as the other, so that man may not find out anything that will be after him Ecclesiastes 7:14

This verse from Ecclesiastes reminds us that God is in ultimate control. When we have good days, it is He who blesses us. When we have days of struggle, He will strengthen us to meet the challenge. Earlier in the devotionals, you read that God often uses struggles to increase our need to turn to Him. He does not send evil our way, but we may be tested by events in our lives. When we have a particularly trying day, God knows what is happening and will help us with our needs when we ask Him. The other very important concept in this verse is that unpredictability is God's way of reminding us to rely on Him. He wants us to trust Him. He knows that mankind has a tendency to not rely on God when things are good. He wants us to rely on Him all of our days. Because only He knows the future, we understand that man cannot know the future. Only God knows what will happen tomorrow, the next day, or the next year. We do not know. We can only trust Him to strengthen and lead us every day.

Do not boast about tomorrow, for you do not know what a day may bring Proverbs 27:1

Caregivers of loved ones with progressively deteriorating conditions have particular trials. This is because of the uncertainty of the progression of the disease, the increasingly significant support needed, and the existing elephant in the room: this disease is not curable. With these considerations in mind, the caregivers of those with these conditions, must remember that a prognosis by a medical staff may be accurate, but the time remaining is known only to God. Some individuals with these conditions live for many years while others may take their heavenly journey in a matter of days or weeks. Only God knows this. How can caregivers cope with these questions?

The Lord will fulfill his purpose for me; your steadfast love, O Lord, endures forever. Do not forsake the work of your hands Psalm 138:8

As the verse from Psalm tells us, we continue to fulfill the purpose that God has for us. Comforting a loved one who receives an unwelcome prognosis about a disease is one reason God placed us in this role. Being there to support our loved one is our goal. For this, we trust and rely on God to guide our path. We know that, no matter what else happens, God endures always. As Christians caring for loved ones with serious health concerns, we are doing the work that God would have us do: care for the weak, the sick, and the disabled. Continue to love and care for your loved one. Read the Scriptures for inspiration and strength. And pray.

Heavenly Father, we cannot know the future. Only you, Father, know our number of days and the joy and pain that each day may bring. Please renew my strength. Help me to be of service to my loved one. Amen.

Terry Overton

When Going to Church Seems Impossible

So then you are no longer strangers and aliens, but you are fellow citizens with the saints and members of the household of God. Built on the foundation of the apostles and prophets, Christ Jesus himself being the cornerstone, in whom the whole structure, being joined together, grows into a holy temple in the Lord. In him you also are being built together into a dwelling place for God by the Spirit Ephesians 2:19-22

If you and your loved one attended church and other Christian fellowship activities before the illness or injury, you might not be able to do so as regularly. There may come a time in the near future when it is impossible to go to your church. But as stated in the verses above written by the Apostle Paul, the church is not really a building.

Think back in history to the time when Paul began his own ministry. At that time, the buildings where people worshiped and prayed were temples and were part of the Jewish faith. You may also remember that the first Christians, including Christ himself, were originally trained in and knew the Jewish faith. The early Christians therefore either worshiped the Scriptures of the Jewish faith in the temples or they worshiped Jesus and met to pray about and discuss their new-found Christian faith in peoples' homes. Jesus met with his earliest followers, the disciples, in small homes and upper rooms of homes. As you notice then, going to a specific building is not required to practice Christianity.

In the verses above, the reader can easily feel the welcoming warmth of the early Christians by Paul's statements. We know that today we gather with other Christians for fellowship. You and your loved one can continue to worship and pray even though going to church is not possible. As noted in earlier devotionals, it will lift your spirit and your loved one's spirit, to invite fellow Christians in to your home, or the home of your loved one, to share Scripture, Bible stories, worship, and pray. Your Pastor may want to participate in such gatherings.

What then, brothers? When you come together, each one has a hymn, a lesson, a revelation, a tongue, or an interpretation. Let all things be done for building up 1 Corinthians 14:26

Meeting together to share fellowship indeed can be an opportunity to lift each other up as you share conversation about your faith. Visiting with others socially can take your mind, and your loved one's mind, off of the trials of the illness and the burden of the daily routines. And remember the purpose of Paul's words to these new believers was to strengthen faith. These believers were new to the Christian faith and sharing time together to strengthen their faith meant that the church would strengthen and grow. As you meet, strive to strengthen your faith and that of the other people who gather with you.

Heavenly Father, I know that the people who believe in You and your Son, Jesus, are the church. Help me to strengthen my own faith and that of others as we meet together. Amen.

Terry Overton

Just Want Things to Be Like They Used to Be

Do not be anxious about anything, but in everything by prayer and supplication with thanksgiving let your requests be made known to God. And the peace of God, which surpasses all understanding, will guard your hearts and minds in Christ Jesus Philippians 4:6-7

You have been managing the health and well-being of your loved one for some time now. There may be days when your mind drifts back to life as it used to be, prior to their illness or injury. You might remember the regular rhythm of your daily life without the numerous visits to a variety of doctors; hospital stays, hospital sitting, treatments, therapies, medication changes, physical assistance, and other requirements of caregiving. At that time, you may have thought your life was busy yet peaceful. Nowadays, your life ebbs and flows between crises and down times and between struggles and small steps of progress. You may just wish things were like they used to be in the past.

There is no turning back. You know that is a fact. Your loved one may make progress eventually and return to work or other daily functions. Or your loved one may be on the long road to heaven. Either way, things have changed significantly, and you have too. You may fluctuate between exhausted and, well, really exhausted. You may have to search each day to find the strength to go on to the next phase or treatment. But you endure.

What can you do, then, to feel better about your circumstance? As the verses above by the Apostle Paul tell us, we should first be thankful and pray and request our needs with thankfulness in our hearts. About this time, you may not remember the many blessings in your life. Remember, the greatest blessing of all was given to us:

For God so loved the world, that he gave his only Son, that whoever believes in him should not perish but have eternal life John 3:16

When you pray, you can begin by first giving thanks for the grace given to us. Then you request what you need to make your day go smoothly: strength, love, patience, and peace. As the verse from Romans states below, when we focus only on our worldly cares, we will not find peace. Set your thoughts on God and the peace we have in Christ Jesus.

For to set the mind on the flesh is death, but to set the mind on the Spirit is life and peace Romans 8:6

Your world will not be the same. It may be that your loved one's world will not change or may even become more challenging. But you can remember the blessings you have with your loved one and cherish these days. Find something to make you, and your loved one, smile today. Spend time with God, breathe in the fresh air, watch birds fly, talk to others you care about, and thank God for your blessings.

Heavenly Father, thank you for the many blessings you provide for us each day. In our time of need, help us to remain at peace in your love and to remember we have joy in Christ Jesus. Amen.

Terry Overton

Deep Depression and Sadness

Answer me quickly, O Lord! My spirit fails! Hide not your face from me, lest I be like those who go down to the pit. Let me hear in the morning of your steadfast love, for in you I trust. Make me know the way I should go, for you I lift up my soul Psalm 143:7-8

The verses from Psalm above, written by David, tell the reader that David is in deep despair. In these verses, it is easy to see that he feels even God has not been reachable. He sounds distressed in his demand that God pays attention to him now, at this very moment. He feels deeply saddened and tells God that his spirit is failing. He longs to know that God is present and demands that God show his face to him, or, in other words, he is asking to sense God's presence. He asks that God let him know that a new day in his faith is coming to him. He wants to know for certain that God will help him. He is trusting God and asks for a sign or some way to know the direction that he should take. He knows that he must depend on God for knowledge about which direction to turn and is lifting up his soul to God for an answer. He does not want to remain in the pit of despair.

You may feel such depression and sadness at times about your loved one that you do not know where to turn for help. Always know that your pastor or counselor will be there for you. Other Christians can provide support. If you feel too depressed to know what to do, reach out to those who can offer you help and support. That is their purpose and how they serve God. Allow them to serve Him as they were called to do. Pray to God and ask that He take you out of the pit of your own despair. You too are called to serve by supporting your loved one. To do this well, you will need to ask others for support so that you can complete your tasks at hand. Pray, talk to those who can support you, and you will be able to leave the pit of despair to serve your loved one with joy in your heart and a renewed spirit.

The Lord is near to the brokenhearted and saves the crushed in spirit Psalm 34:18

This verse from Psalm, written by David, reminds us once again that God is near. David tells others that he knows God has helped others who were in despair. God is always with you. You must take His hand, ask Him to lift you up. He will save you from your despair. He is waiting for you to ask Him for help.

Let not your hearts be troubled. Believe in God; believe also in me John 14:1

Jesus told us himself, in this verse from the book of John, we are not to let our hearts be heavy or in despair, but we should believe in God the Father and the Son. By believing always, we can rejoice in our final victory and remain at peace in our hearts.

Heavenly Father, thank you for sending your Son so that we may have hope and our hearts may be lifted up. My heart has been heavy, and my soul is in despair. Please give me strength and hope as You lift my heart. Amen.

Terry Overton

When You Think It Can't Get Worse, It Does

In all your ways acknowledge him, and he will make straight your paths Proverbs 3:6

Some days, no matter how hard you try to give the needed care to your loved one, nothing goes right. It might have nothing to do with your actual caring for the loved one, but other unexpected things happen. You load up your loved one to go to the arranged doctor's appointment or therapy session only to notice a flat tire. Once you arrange for transportation and to get the flat tire repaired, you are off to the appointment and then arrive without the proper insurance papers. You try to call someone for help and realize your cell phone is inside your house. You left the phone when you called for the tire repair. And, so it goes. Your efforts are not getting you anywhere. Nothing is going as planned for the day. You finally make it home and find a bill in the mail that you overlooked, and, just at that time, the phone rings. Before you pick up the phone, you hear a crash as your loved one calls out for your help in the other room. This is a day with a series of calamities!

The verse from Proverbs reminds us that if we acknowledge God always, that He will make our paths straight. But on days when nothing goes right, it is hard to understand how your path is straight. You seem to be spinning your wheels and going in circles. It is at this time that we need to remember what is written in Hebrews. Jesus is always the same. If we are struggling, frustrated, angry, upset, nervous, or just exhausted from dealing with the mishaps of the day, we can turn to God for peace.

Jesus Christ is the same yesterday and today and forever Hebrews 13:8

Say a prayer. Take a few minutes to gather your thoughts. And read Scriptures, like the verses below from Habakkuk:

Though the fig tree should not blossom, nor fruit be on the vines, the produce of the olive fail and the fields yield no food, the flock be cut off from the fold, and there be no herd in the stalls, yet I will rejoice in the Lord; I will take joy in the God of my salvation. God, the Lord, is my strength; he makes my fee like the deer's; he makes me tread on my high places Habakkuk 3:17-19

Remembering that God is always near and can provide you with inner peace, even when your world seems to be coming unglued at the seams, can bring you relief from the frustration and exasperation. Thinking about these things, arm yourself. You can get through this day. God is with you always. Stand firm.

Therefore take up the whole armor of God, that you may be able to withstand in the evil day, and having done all, to stand firm Ephesians 6:13

Heavenly Father, thank you for your peace and strength. Remind me that You are always beside me and offer me peace in times when things are chaotic. Amen.

Terry Overton

Walking Through the Shadow of the Valley

For God gave us a spirit not of fear but of power and love and self-control 2 Timothy 1:7

Caregivers of loved ones with terminal or progressive illnesses may find that this disease will cast an ominous cloud over you for many days. You may know that ultimately the disease will take your loved one and that their journey to their heavenly home is in the near future. Knowing this may become the lens through which you observe everything. This will cast great despair over your days, and your mood will be detected by your loved one.

Caregivers of loved ones without terminal illnesses may nevertheless have feelings of anxiousness when loved ones have surgeries or severe treatments for their conditions. The condition of the loved one may mean the loved one has a predisposition to other illnesses or conditions that can cause harm. A disabled loved one who falls and breaks a hip is at risk for a host of other problems. A loved one who must have prolonged hospital stays is also in jeopardy of contracting unwanted infections or viruses that can be disastrous.

These scenarios can bring anxiety and worry into your mind frequently. There are many things to consider about the future while you are caring for your loved one and plenty of opportunities to agonize about the impending or possible outcome. How can you best deal with the worry? The Apostle Paul wrote to Timothy, his younger fellow believer whom he mentored in a letter, 2 Timothy. In the verse above, Paul tells Timothy not to worry because God has given humans a spirit that is powerful, full of love, and capable of self-control. When you are feeling like your emotions are coming unhinged, how can you feel control? No doubt it is difficult to remember the words Paul wrote when you are feeling out of control yourself. But this is the time to remember who is in control. It will be God's timing when any of us take our heavenly journey home.

DEVOTIONAL FOR THOSE COPING WITH TRAGEDY

When there is nothing you can do to control a situation, it is time to put your worry in God's hands completely. To help you turn this over to God, remember that nothing will ever separate you or your loved one from Christ.

For I am sure that neither death nor life, nor angels nor rulers, nor things present nor things to come, nor powers, nor height or depth, nor anything else in all creation, will be able to separate us from the love of God in Christ Jesus our Lord Romans 8:38-39

Always remember, you and your loved one, are in God's hands. We live by His clock, not our own. For today, spend time with your loved one and appreciate the opportunities you have to care for and love your loved one and your family.

Heavenly Father, only You know the time we will journey to heaven. Thank you for the peace You give me by loving me and giving me the strength to serve my loved one. Amen.

Family Distancing and Differences

And if it is evil in your eyes to serve the Lord, choose this day whom you will serve, whether the gods your fathers served in the region beyond the River, or the gods of the Amorites in whose land you dwell. But as for me and my house, we will serve the Lord Joshua 24:15

The book of Joshua depicts a long struggle between Joshua and some of the people of Israel who were tempted to worship other gods. In several verses in chapter 24, Joshua reminds the people that God had been protecting the people of Israel for a long time. They were the chosen people of God. He states, one of the most quoted verses from this book, that he and his house would serve God.

When your family initially learned of the illness or the condition of your loved one, they likely called, visited, or volunteered to assist you in the caregiving. As time goes on, weeks to months or months to years, family members may drift away. You may even have disagreements with some members of your family about the strategies you use to serve your loved one or the treatment you or your loved one selected. You may have disagreements about visiting, joining in family activities, or even support and resources. These types of interactions can be annoying and even maddening.

It is hurtful for your loved one to witness these discussions or to have other family members complain about your efforts. Your loved one can become upset or even more ill if tensions persist. Should these discussions go on for an extended period, your loved one will suffer from long-term conflicts. This may impact their overall quality of life.

Your family members may seldom come to visit or stop coming over for visits altogether. Perhaps you have called and invited the other family members to come by on numerous occasions. The family members may say they are too busy or say they are coming and never show up. Not only is this challenging to deal with, but it can cause sadness and worry in your loved one.

Remember that you are serving God by serving your loved one. You may need to step back and think about how all of these interactions can have a positive outcome. If it is evident that the family will not be involved with your loved one in a helpful way, it is time to put your loved one's feelings first and attempt to fill in the gaps with happiness. Ask the loved one if there is some activity they would like to do on specific days or set a date to take a short excursion. Spend quality time doing something interactive and enjoyable together. When you are exhausted, ask God to help you through each day.

Families are complicated. There is no magical TV family in which all the members live together in harmony, placing each one's wishes ahead of their own. But you can have harmony in your own environment by always putting God first and serving your loved one as you know He would want.

You will also find peace yourself if you can forgive your family members and thank God that you are the one spending these important days with your loved one. Even though you and your family members may disagree, you are still family. You have love in your heart for them that will be there when things settle down. Do not engage in angry interactions that will increase negative emotions and tension. Always turn to the love from Christ Jesus to remember how He would have us treat each other.

A new commandment I give to you, that you love one another; just as I have loved you, you also are to love one another. By this all people will know that you are my disciples, if you have love for one another John 13:34-35

Heavenly Father, thank you for showing me how to live by sending your Son as an example for me. In my tough days, please give me strength and peace in my heart. Help me to provide cheerful care to my loved one. Amen.

I Am Here for You (Even When I Need Some Rest)

But ask the beasts, and they will teach you; the birds of the heavens, and they will tell you; or the bushes of the earth, and they will teach you; and the fish of the sea will declare to you. Who among all of these does not know that the hand of the Lord has done this? In his hand is the life of every living thing and the breath of all mankind Job 12:7-10

You know of Job's struggles. He suffered greatly for a long period of time. His faith was strong even in his weaknesses. The verses above are part of a conversation he was having with his friends. He was proving his point to his friends that even the animals and all creation know that everything is in God's hands. This includes His knowledge of our suffering and His strength and guidance to lead us through our trials.

Caregivers become weak, weary, and downtrodden. The work of a caregiver is like no other. Being a caregiver of a newborn infant is demanding, but in caring for a typically developing infant, there is knowledge of growing, improving skills, learning, laughing, and becoming independent. In the work of a caregiver, there may be a loss of skills, independence, and plenty of frustration and crying. In a child with a disabling condition, the pain may grow as they do, when you realize the stark differences between other children and your child's condition. In those with progressive diseases or conditions, you witness deterioration. The days are not filled with anticipation of progressing to the next joyful step of independence.

As you read in earlier devotionals and have probably experienced in depth, caregiving is lonely work at times. When you need someone else there to assist you with moving your loved one from point A to point B, there is no help. When you wish someone else could change the linens or fix a meal, there is no help. Day after day of this work and loneliness is grueling. You feel drained.

Your loved knows that you are giving yourself to meet their needs. Your work does not go unnoticed by your loved one, or by God. But even so, some days you think you are too tired to go on. You would like and need, more rest. But somehow, amazingly, when your loved one calls you, you are on your feet again. You may go days without a "thank you" or "I am glad you are here helping me." But you are doing the work that Jesus said we should do. When He was speaking to followers about how judgment would be determined by God, He said the following verses written in Matthew:

Then the King will say to those on his right, "Come you who are blessed by my Father, inherit the kingdom prepared for you from the fountain of the world. For I was hungry and you gave me food, I was thirsty and you gave me drink, I was a stranger and you welcomed me, I was naked and you clothed me, I was sick and you visited me, I was in prison and you came to me. Then the righteous will answer him, saying, 'Lord when did we see you hungry and feed you, or thirsty and give you drink? And when did we see you a stranger and welcome you, or naked and clothe you? And when did we see you sick or in prison and visit you?' And the King will answer them, "Truly, I say to you, as you did for the least of these my brothers, you did it to me" Matthew 25:34-40

Caregiving is doing exactly what Jesus would have you do. He knows that you are the one who can meet the needs of your loved one. He knows the love and determination you have in your heart. These are the days of digging deep into your heart, your mind, and your energy stores. These are the days of putting a smile on your tired face, rolling up your sleeves, and giving it the best you have. For this endurance and strength, remember another verse from Matthew:

But Jesus looked at them and said, "With man this is impossible, but with God all things are possible" Matthew 19:26

Heavenly Father, thank you for giving me the strength I need. I am pleased to be the caregiver of my loved one. Continue to give me strength and endurance to follow the example set by Jesus. Amen.

God is Here

Am I a God at hand, declares the Lord, and not a God far away? Can a man hide himself in secret places so that I cannot see him? Declares the Lord. Do I not fill heaven and earth? Declares the Lord Jeremiah 23:23-24

The verse above by Jeremiah is one in which God tells us He can be with us even when we think we are far away from Him. He told Jeremiah that He is everywhere in heaven and earth. There is no place, no hospital room, no waiting room, no dark middle of the night moment when you are helping your loved one to bed, in which God is not present. For believers in God, He is with us always.

There may be days you are overcome, overwhelmed, and overextended when you do not sense His presence. On those days, in the darkness of a tired night, you may have to seek Him. This you do by calming your heart and mind. Read Bible verses if you are not too weary. Say quiet prayers to God from your inner heart. Seek Him.

But from there you will seek the Lord your God and you will find him, if you search after him with all your heart and with all your soul Deuteronomy 4:29

In the verse from Deuteronomy above, God inspired Moses to tell the people of Israel that they must continue to seek God. The people strayed, and in this book, we see that God does not tolerate false prophets or teaching. He tells Moses that He is present, but the people must seek Him only.

For caregivers who feel they cannot sense God's presence, it is helpful to read Scripture, pray, and think about God's grace and peace. Pray for strength and guidance to bring you back to your faith and to feel God's presence. Pray for the strength of continuing to care for your loved one as Christ cared for those whom believed in Him.

But you have upheld me because of my integrity, and set me in your presence forever Psalm 41:12

David wrote this part of Psalm when he had been battling many different issues. He knew that even in the mist of trials, because he held firmly to God and his faith, God would continue to bless and keep David in His presence. Caregivers face trial after trial and must keep their faith strong. Seek God's presence.

Heavenly Father, thank you for being in my world. Help me always to remember your presence and to seek you when I am feeling weak in my faith. Amen.

Recalibration of Happiness

I perceived that there is nothing better for them than to be joyful and to do good as long as they live Ecclesiastes 3:12-13

As Christians, we may wonder about our part in God's bigger plan for our lives. Worrying about the future and the caring of our loved one in the future may cause us to take our eyes off of the larger vision that God has for us. In the verses above from Ecclesiastes, Solomon tells people that there is nothing better for us to think about or to do than good works. He adds that we should continue these good works all of the days of our lives.

As a caregiver, you can take joy in the work you do each day. There is no greater gift to a person than to take care of them when they cannot take care of themselves. Who else would they turn to? They have turned to you. This may be a matter of preference, or necessity, that you are their caregiver. In any case, taking pleasure in your work is pleasing to God and to your loved one. For some time, then, your happiness may be measured by a different metric. You are no longer concerned with worldly achievements. You are now focused on providing a loving and supportive environment for your loved one.

In the verse below, again Solomon tells the people that they should rejoice in their work for that is what has been planned for them to do. He reminds the people that there is no way to see beyond what they are currently doing in this life. It is a reminder once again that we cannot know God's plans. Only God can determine what lies ahead for us.

So I saw that there is nothing better than that a man should rejoice in his work, for that is his lot. Who can bring him to see what will be after him? Ecclesiastes 3:22

Caregivers may have many days of inconvenience as they provide service to a loved one. As you read in earlier devotionals, priorities change, your world becomes smaller and more focused, and you may be exhausted and feel lonely. The Apostle Paul suffered greatly for his work for Christ. He was tortured, chased, and beaten. Remember the words of the Apostle Paul below about his ability to find contentment during rough times:

For the sake of Christ, then, I am content with weaknesses, insults, hardships, persecutions, and calamities. For when I am weak, then I am strong 2 Corinthians 12:10

When you begin to feel frustration, fatigue, or despair, remember how others have suffered and found their peace through the words of Christ Jesus.

Heavenly Father, thank you for reminding me of contentment through Christ Jesus and reading your inspired words. Help me to know peace and the contentment of serving my loved one. Amen.

Frustration

And let us not grow weary of doing good, for in due season we will reap, if we do not give up Galatians 6:9

It no doubt can be exhausting and frustrating to continue the caregiving tasks day after day. It is also exasperating to work so hard and not receive a word of thanks or acknowledgment. But you must continue. As you have read in other devotionals, take a break when possible. However, after an extended period of time, even breaks may not be as helpful as before. What are you to do?

This is the time for much-needed fellowship with others. Think about someone you can call to come over for a cup of coffee or visit with on the phone. Even when you feel frustration, you will continue to do the right thing for your loved one. That much you know. And you also know you will not give up even though it is a very long road you are traveling. Like other devotionals you have read, you know that it is easier to share the burden, even if only sharing socially. Feelings of exhaustion, frustration, and not being appreciated can mount up. Don't let them. Address these feelings when you sense that you are becoming overtired.

In the verse above written by the Apostle Paul to the Galatians, he encouraged them to continue even though they did not obtain a reward at the present time. He reminded these new believers that their reward would eventually be theirs in Christ Jesus. At times when you feel frustration and exhaustion, ask God for the strength and peacefulness of heart to continue your work.

Therefore lift your drooping hands and strengthen your weak knees, and make straight paths for your feet so that what is lame may not be put out of joint but rather be healed. Strive for peace with everyone, and for the holiness without which no one will see the Lord Hebrews 12:12-14

You probably have also felt your drooping hands and weak knees, but as the verse above tells us, we are to continue to walk the straight path and to get along with others. At this time, you may find the company of other Christians especially helpful. Remember that we are charged to look after each other. Fellow Christians may be useful in relieving the stress and providing you with a needed break. Ask other family members to assist by giving you a respite so that you can be refreshed to take care of your loved one. And pray for strength and patience. Always cherish the days you have with your loved one.

Heavenly Father, thank you for providing me with the strength to serve my loved one for all of this period of time. Please help me now to endure and to rest in your peace. Amen.

For Loved Ones with Terminal Diseases

In my Father's house are many rooms. If it were not so, would I have told you that I go to prepare a place for you? John 14:2

You likely recognize the verse above as a quote from Jesus to the disciples. He was talking with the disciples before He faced crucifixion. He knew what was coming. The disciples believed strongly in Jesus, but they did not really understand what He was telling them. The disciples did not know how Jesus would die. They certainly did not understand the resurrection until it happened. But here, Jesus wanted them to know that something was about to happen that would change everything. Yet, they were not to worry because He was going to be crucified for them and then, later, they would join Him. He was going ahead to make a place for the disciples and for all believers.

In many ways, humans have the same worries and anxieties about death. We do not know how it will happen, but we know it will. If your loved one has a terminal illness, one that will eventually take them to their heavenly home, you do not know exactly when or how that will happen. These are matters that only God knows. Like the disciples, we know that we are not to worry, but it is often difficult to face death and not worry about the details.

Even for those who have suffered months, or years, with terminal diseases, we are not "ready" for the disease to take its toll. Watching the deterioration over such an extended period may find you praying for relief for your loved one. You pray for relief from pain, sorrow, worry. And when death comes, you are unprepared.

The sorrow will come, and now the pain will be yours. You will feel the pain in your heart because the life you were sharing with your loved one, caring, supporting, and encouraging them through it all, is over. You will feel the void in your own heart.

DEVOTIONAL FOR THOSE COPING WITH TRAGEDY

It will be challenging to feel peace and joy in your heart. You know your loved one is no longer suffering from pain and you will tell yourself that over and over. But you will mourn. This is the time for you to look for support. Look to your family, friends, other Christians, and your pastor. Always look to the Scripture for comfort and to keep your faith strong.

In the verse below, Jesus was comforting His disciples because they were worried about what He was telling them about His impending death. He comforted them by telling them they would see Him again and the joy would be amazing. He explained that the joy would be astounding and no one would be able to take that joy away.

Think about your loved one making the final journey and know that all Christians will have eternal life in heaven.

So also you have sorrow now, but I will see you again, and your hearts will rejoice, and no one will take your joy from you John 16:22

Heavenly Father, thank you for blessing my life by giving me my loved one. Please help my heart to be strong and to remain steadfast in faith. Amen.

Rejoicing Always

But we see him who for a little while was made lower than the angels, namely Jesus, crowned with glory and honor because of the suffering of death, so that by the Grace of God he might taste death for everyone Hebrews 2:9

Your role as caregiver for this long period has been one of toil, patience, endurance, and perhaps grief. Through all of your trials, you know that Christians celebrate the gift of grace and eternal life granted by the death and resurrection of Christ Jesus. This is true always, even on the days when you can think of nothing else to celebrate. Rejoice in the knowledge that God the Father has taken care of you, and your loved one, by giving the greatest gift of all. For this, we can always rejoice through pain, sorrow, and frustration.

Perhaps your loved one has experienced or will soon experience their heavenly birth. For many days following this event, you may feel great sorrow. As humans, this is a perfectly natural response. Your loved one is no longer with you to share your time. As Christians, we know that God has planned this life cycle for us so that we can eventually have eternal peace and joy. Our body may be placed into the earth, but our spirit is in God's hands.

And the dust to returns to the earth as it was, and the spirit returns to God who gave it Ecclesiastes 12:7

In this you rejoice, though now for a little while, if necessary, you have been grieved by various trials 1 Peter 1:6

So as the days follow one after another, you continue through your life with the memories of your precious loved one for whom you cared and supported in their time of need. Your sadness will lessen a little each day until you notice that you are feeling better, holding on to the faith in Christ Jesus that your loved one is at peace.

You may have a time of great need in the future. No doubt during your caregiving experience you questioned what your own fate might be in the future. All of these worries and questions are already known to God, in whose hands we place our faith, love, and hope. Therefore, because we have God and His Son in our hearts, we can always rejoice no matter what else we may be experiencing in life. Remember that for all believers in the grace granted by Christ Jesus, we will join our wonderful loving Savior at the appointed time. At that time, we will rejoice beyond understanding by earthly measures. Be thankful for the opportunity to walk the path of a caregiver while holding on to God's hand.

You make known to me the path of life; in your presence there is fulness of joy; at your right hand are pleasures forevermore Psalm 16:11

Heavenly Father, thank you for the wonderful gift of eternal life You have given to me through your Son, Christ Jesus. Thank you for the blessed opportunity to be a caregiver for my loved one. Grant me peace and help me to rejoice in Your love always. Amen.

Afterword

Dear Reader,

Your role of the caregiver may continue beyond the days you have read this devotional book. Continue to rely on the Scripture, pray, and strive to feel the joy in your heart each day that is given to us by Christ Jesus. Return to the topics in this devotional that you find helpful. Turn to the Topical Table for Caregivers in the Appendix to locate specific verses used for the topics in this devotional.

If your loved one has experienced their final journey home, please know that I mourn with you in your loss. Pray for strength to continue your own life path. Participate in fellowship with your family, friends, and other Christians, who will support you at this time.

Blessings to you and your family,

Terry Overton

Appendix

Topical Table for Caregivers		
Topic	Title of Devotional	Scripture
Learning About the Loved One's Condition	Nothing is the Same: The Day Our Worlds Changed	Joshua 1:9 Psalm 119:114
Handling and Understanding Information from Doctors	Doctors Reports	Galatians 6:2 Psalm 25:4-5
Denial/Disbelief	Disbelief	Jeremiah 29:11 Deuteronomy 31:8
Why Did this Happen to Us?	Why? The Unanswered Question	Proverbs 3:5 Isaiah 55:9 1 Chronicles 16:11
Your Difficult Role	Crossing the Turbulent Sea	Isaiah 43:2 Psalm 54:4
Rejoicing in God	Light in the Darkness	Psalm 118:24 1 John 4:18 Psalm 5:11
Loved One Does Not Comprehend; Alzheimer's, Stroke, Coma, Medications	Eyes Looking But Not Knowing	2 Corinthians 5:7 Hebrews 11:1

Topical Table for Caregivers		
Topic	Title of Devotional	Scripture
Feeling Abandoned	Am I Alone?	Deuteronomy 31:6 James 5:13
When Loved Ones Can't Talk to You	Wondering About Their Thoughts	Psalm 46:10 John 14:27
When Loved Ones Have Physical Challenges	Struggling to Get Around Physically	Luke 14:12-12 Philippians 2:4
Feeling Lonely in Caregiving	Everyday Loneliness	1 Peter 5:8 Psalm 40:16
Staying positive	Hope	Romans 8:24-25 Psalm 39:7 Psalm 71:14
Sadness and Depression in Caregiving	Sadness	Psalm 34:18 2 Corinthians 4:8-9
Fellowship with Christians	Who Do You Turn To?	Colossians 2:2 Matthew 18:20
Giving and Receiving Positive Comments	How Can You Talk to People?	1 Thessalonians 5:11 Psalm 54:4

Topical Table for Caregivers		
Topic	Title of Devotional	Scripture
God is With You Always	Loneliness	Psalm 38:9 1 John 4:23
Doubled Responsibilities	What Was Once Done by Two Must Now Be Done by One	Hebrews 12:11 Luke 14:28
Strength to Carry On	So Tired...God Please Give Me Energy	Matthew 11:28-30 Isaiah 40:31
Faith	Faith	1 Corinthians 2:5 Romans 10:17 Hebrews 11:6
Tests in Our Lives	Joy in Suffering	James 1:2-4 James 1:12 Psalm 28:71 Corinthians 2:5
Lack of Freedom	Feeling Imprisoned	Philippians 2:14 2 Corinthians 3:17 Psalm 118:5
Interactions with Others	Letting Professionals Do Their Job	Proverbs 12:15 Proverbs 19:20 John 17:4

Topical Table for Caregivers		
Topic	Title of Devotional	Scripture
Other Person Always First	Priorities Change	Colossians 3:2 James 3:13 1 John 4:19
Mad at God	Feeling Anger Toward God	Job 27:2 Romans 12:9
Unfamiliar Decisions	New Decisions	2 Timothy 1:13 Proverbs 15:22 2 Thessalonians 3:13
Regret	Things I Wish I Had Said	Ecclesiastes 7:10 Proverbs 16:33 Ecclesiastes 5:20
Nights without Sleep	Longest Nights	2 Corinthians 11:27 Philippians 4:6-7 Jeremiah 31:25
Less Exposure to My Previous World	Smaller World	Romans 8:18 Psalm 34:19
Keeping Hope in Your Heart	Helpless but Not Without Hope	Romans 15:4 Psalm 34:15 Romans 15:13

DEVOTIONAL FOR THOSE COPING WITH TRAGEDY

Topical Table for Caregivers		
Topic	Title of Devotional	Scripture
Time is Short	Time to Get Everything Done	James 4:13-15 Psalm 90:12 Psalm 90:15
Need for Family to Help	Family Support	1Thessalonians 5:14 Philippians 1:6
Financial Concerns	Resources to Meet Our Needs	Philippians 4:11-12 Philippians 4:19
Depression	Nothing to Smile About	Psalm 23: 1-6 Psalm 3:3
Loved One Can't Talk	No Talking, No Sharing	Psalm 71:9 Hebrews 4:12 Psalm 90:10
Feeling weak and tired	Physical Dependence on Others	Isaiah 40:29 Psalm 121:3 Psalm 73:26
Walking, Talking Dressing, Feeding Skills	Basic Skills	James 3:1 Ephesians 6:7 Luke 6:31
Struggling to Hang On	No One Knows What I'm Going Through	1 Thessalonians 5:18

Topical Table for Caregivers		
Topic	Title of Devotional	Scripture
		Hebrews 13:16 Ephesians 6:10
Happiness	Finding Joy in Little Things	Philippians 4:4 Psalm 33:21 John 15:9-11 Psalm 4:7
Getting Enough Rest	A Minute to Sit Down	Exodus 34:21 Ecclesiastes 4:6 Psalm 127:2 Proverbs 3:24
Ungratefulness	When Your Efforts are Not Appreciated	Psalm 100:1-5 Philippians 2:3-4
Change in Personality	A Different Person	1 Samuel 16:7 Romans 7:15
Instability of Mood	Roller Coaster Emotions	Proverbs 29:11 Romans 12:15 1 Peter 4:8
Self-care of Caregiver	Finding Time to Take Care of the Caregiver	1 Corinthians 6:19-20 Psalm 118:5-6

DEVOTIONAL FOR THOSE COPING WITH TRAGEDY

Topical Table for Caregivers		
Topic	Title of Devotional	Scripture
		Hebrews 6:9-10
Watching Your Loved One Suffer	Watching My Loved One Suffer	Romans 8:26-28 Psalm 119:76
Strengthen Faith	Wanting Answers	James 1:6 Colossians 1:9
Stability of Loved One	Changes in Medications	Isaiah 40:8 Psalm 55:22
Conflict with "Do Gooders"	Well Meaning Advice	James 1:5 James 3:17
Changes in Personnel	Adjusting to Different Caregivers	Proverbs 16:2-3 2 Timothy 3:16-17
Loved One Not Cooperative	Refusing Help	Luke 12:12 Proverbs 18:15 Proverbs 119:66
Falls and Other Mishaps	Accidents Happen	Psalm 139:13-14 Job 10:8-12 Job 42:1-3
Quality of Life Questions	Quality of Life	Psalm 119:50 Psalm 73:26 John 5:24 John 11:25

Topical Table for Caregivers		
Topic	Title of Devotional	Scripture
Endurance and Faith	Strength to Go Through the Next Phase	Hebrews 2:1 Ephesians 4:2
Faith Questions	Is It too Late to Grow Faith?	Jeremiah 6:16 Romans 14:1 John 1:12
Peace	Peace	2 Thessalonians 3:16 1 Peter 5:7 Philippians 4:9
Memory Loss	Being the Memory for Those Who Can't Remember	Isaiah 50:4 Hebrews 4:16
Prognosis	Prognosis	Ecclesiastes 7:14 Proverbs 27:1 Psalm 138:8
Christian Gathering	When Going to Church Seems Impossible	Ephesians 2:19-22 1 Corinthians 14:26
Thinking about the past	Just Want Things to Be Like They Used to Be	Philippians 4:6-7 John 3:16 Romans 8:6

Topical Table for Caregivers

Topic	Title of Devotional	Scripture
Sadness and depression	Deep Depression and Sadness	Psalm 143:7-8 Psalm 38:18 John 14:1
Dealing with Frustration	When You Think It Can't Get Worse, It Does	Proverbs 3:6 Hebrews 13:8 Habakkuk 3:17-19 Ephesians 6:13
Anxiety of Death	Walking Through the Shadow of The Valley	2 Timothy 1:7 Romans 8:38-39
Family Conflicts	Family Distancing and Differences	Joshua 24:15 John 13:34-35
Exhaustion and endurance	I am Here for You (Even When I Need Some Rest)	Job 12:7-10 Matthew 25:34-40 Matthew 19:26
God is near	God is Here	Jeremiah 23:23-24 Deuteronomy 4:29 Psalm 41:12
Contentment	Recalibration of Happiness	Ecclesiastes 3:12-13 2 Corinthians 12:10

Topical Table for Caregivers		
Topic	Title of Devotional	Scripture
Frustration and exhaustion	Frustration	Galatians 6:9 Hebrews 12:12-14
Anxiety About Death	For Loved Ones with Terminal Diseases	John 14:2 John 16:22
Ending Caregiver Responsibilities	Rejoicing Always	Hebrews 2:9 Ecclesiastes 12:7 1 Peter 1:6 Psalm 16:11

OTHER RELEVANT BOOKS

"Rejoice, young person, while you are young, and let your heart be glad in the days of your youth."
— Wise King Solomon

DEVOTIONAL FOR YOUTHS
GROWING UP IN CHRIST

Terry Overton

Christian Publishing House
ISBN-13: 978-1-945757-90-7
ISBN-10: 1-945757-90-6

Christian Publishing House
ISBN-13: 978-1-945757-92-1
ISBN-10: 1-945757-92-2

DEVOTIONAL FOR THOSE COPING WITH TRAGEDY

"ALL SCRIPTURE IS INSPIRED BY GOD AND PROFITABLE FOR TEACHING, FOR REPROOF, FOR CORRECTION, FOR TRAINING IN RIGHTEOUSNESS"—2 TIMOTHY 3:16

REASONABLE FAITH

Saving Those Who Doubt

EDWARD D. ANDREWS

Christian Publishing House
ISBN-13: 978-1-945757-91-4
ISBN-10: 1-945757-91-4

Christian Publishing House
ISBN-13: 978-1-945757-47-1
ISBN-10: 1-945757-47-7

DEVOTIONAL FOR THOSE COPING WITH TRAGEDY

Christian Publishing House
ISBN-13: 978-1-945757-60-0
ISBN-10: 1-945757-60-4

Terry Overton

Christian Publishing House
ISBN-13: 978-1-945757-42-6
ISBN-10: 1-945757-42-6

DEVOTIONAL FOR THOSE COPING WITH TRAGEDY

Christian Publishing House
ISBN-13: 978-1-945757-72-3
ISBN-10: 1-945757-72-8

Terry Overton

Christian Publishing House
ISBN-13: 978-1-945757-69-3
ISBN-10: 1-945757-69-8

DEVOTIONAL FOR THOSE COPING WITH TRAGEDY

Christian Publishing House
ISBN-13: 978-1-945757-74-7
ISBN-10: 1-945757-74-4

Terry Overton

Christian Publishing House
ISBN-13: 978-1-945757-73-0
ISBN-10: 1-945757-73-6

DEVOTIONAL FOR THOSE COPING WITH TRAGEDY

Christian Publishing House
ISBN-13: 978-1-945757-86-0
ISBN-10: 1-945757-86-8

Terry Overton

Christian Publishing House
ISBN-13: 978-1-945757-87-7

ISBN-10: 1-945757-87-6

DEVOTIONAL FOR THOSE COPING WITH TRAGEDY

Christian Publishing House
ISBN-13: 978-1-945757-88-4
ISBN-10: 1-945757-88-4

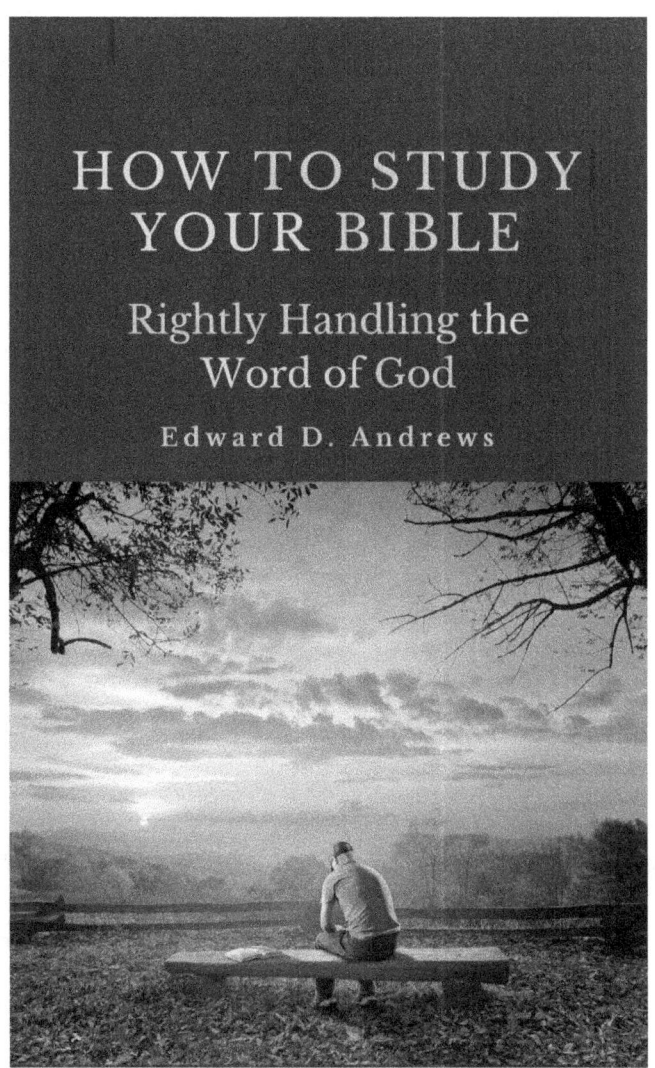

HOW TO STUDY YOUR BIBLE
Rightly Handling the Word of God
Edward D. Andrews

Christian Publishing House
ISBN-13: 978-1-945757-62-4
ISBN-10: 1-945757-62-0

DEVOTIONAL FOR THOSE COPING WITH TRAGEDY

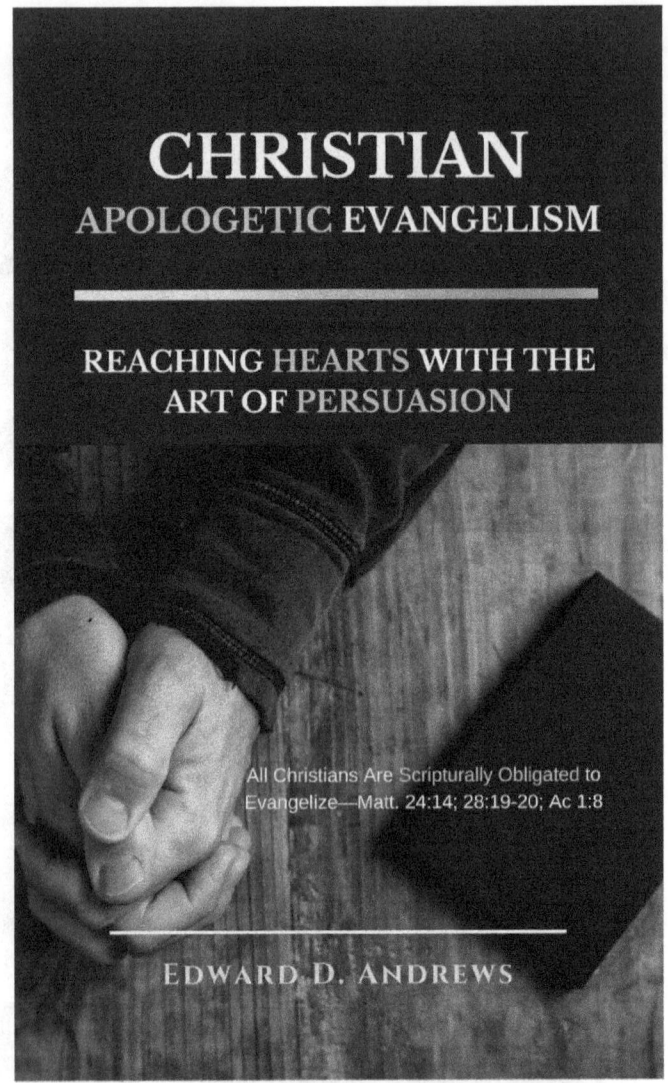

Christian Publishing House
ISBN-13: 978-1-945757-75-4
ISBN-10: 1-945757-75-2

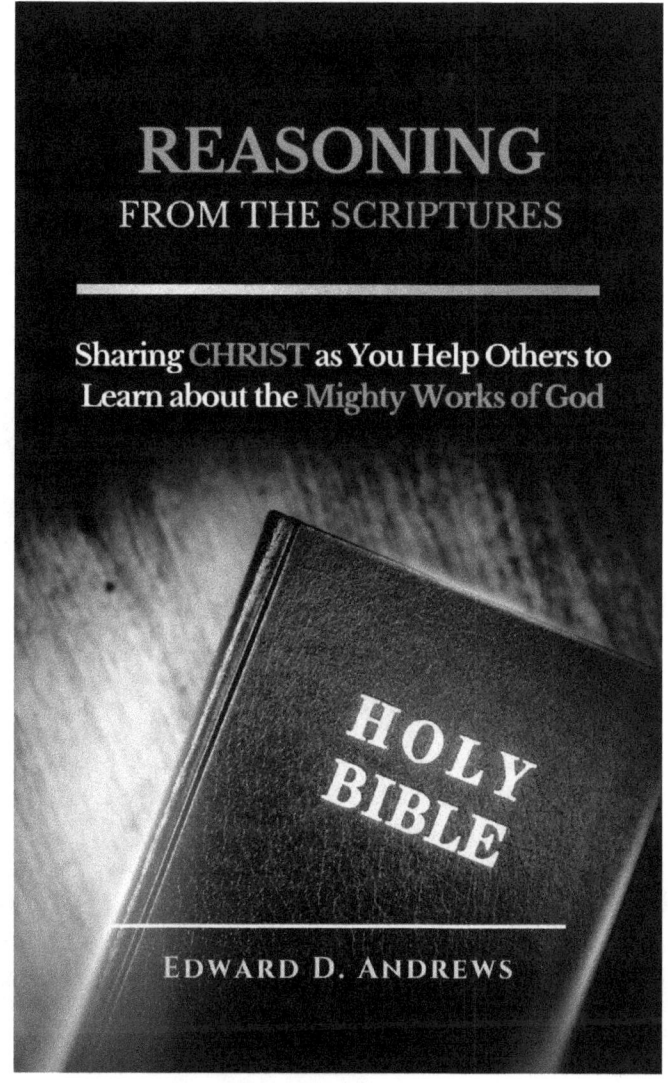

Christian Publishing House
ISBN-13: 978-1-945757-82-2
ISBN-10: 1-945757-75-2

DEVOTIONAL FOR THOSE COPING WITH TRAGEDY

Christian Publishing House
ISBN-13: 978-1-945757-35-8
ISBN-10: 1-945757-35-3

Terry Overton

Christian Publishing House
ISBN-13: 978-1-945757-43-3
ISBN-10: 1-945757-43-4

www.ingramcontent.com/pod-product-compliance
Lightning Source LLC
Chambersburg PA
CBHW060154050426
42446CB00013B/2812